HEAVEN

HEAVEN

BEHOLD!

I MAKE

ALL THINGS

NEW

Robert C. Sutter

authorHOUSE®

AuthorHouse™
1663 Liberty Drive
Bloomington, IN 47403
www.authorhouse.com
Phone: 1-800-839-8640

First published by AuthorHouse   07/08/2011

ISBN: 978-1-4634-2120-5 (sc)
ISBN: 978-1-4634-2119-9 (ebk)

Library of Congress Control Number: 2011910552

Printed in the United States of America

Contents

Acknowledgements

Thanks to

OnLine Bible

Published by

Larry Pierce

King James text includes Strong's numbers

With Greek & Hebrew words defined.

The Value of a Scriptural
Knowledge
Of
Heaven
Candid Warning

It would be less than forthright not to be very candid "upfront" as to the content of this book. So, it is important that the reader read this section first and thereby establish whether or not the topic pertains to them. It could be a waste of time and money to some. To those in the Body of Christ it will be a great incentive to mature as a priest and ministers, not just for time, but for eternity. No doubt that is why God gave it.

It should be clear here that not all who talk of heaven are going there. When thus stated, there is a danger of "shouting fire in a crowded room" and causing panic. That danger in this day is most unlikely. Hell has been "shouted from the rafters" for centuries and has almost universally been discounted, so to many heaven is "neverland, myth, and fairy stories" and won't panic any one. Neither will the other stark realities.

Let's explore the groups that many find this topic of heaven interesting.

Effect on Unrighteous and Ungodly

There are the honest pagans. The Book of Romans depicts them as 1-0f-3 components of a lost human race. Unrighteous and ungodly, and they don't make any bones about it. Well, there is nothing in this book for them or maybe there is. These are the ones He commonly saves.

Effect on the Religious (self-righteous)

The other two segments of a lost race are the self-righteous and religious. They have their separate distinctions, however, here they will be lumped together in the term "religion." Religion in a sinful world has its place. It can be good or bad. It keeps a totally depraved race from being as bad as it could be. It is, however, not part of God's present design. What ever their activity, it will never impede or advance the program of God in this world or beyond. This book deals with the "beyond". Religion does sell a lot of religious books for a multiple number of reasons, Intellect, pleasing God, monetary, debate, culture, bias, to just name a few. Heaven for the religious is a fleshly, earned place and has nothing to do with the Heaven of scripture. What religion likes to do here and how they do it is totally incompatible with what is happening in the scriptural concept of heaven in this book. The only thing this book will do is disrupt the religious on one hand, but on the other hand might just be the convicting tool of the Spirit to extradite a soul from the ranks of the religious.

Effect on the Body of Christ

To those in the Body of Christ there is a multiple blessing in having a scriptural knowledge of heaven. These blessings are an incentive for learning the procedures of ministering in a universal priesthood of believers. Not clergy and laity but universal ministry with no spectators. It conveys the practical, tangible reason for our training here for a practical, tangible functioning there. Heaven is designed for the men God designed, trained and will command in a tangible place with a set objective that will be familiar to them. This answers the "pie in the sky", myths, fairy stories, wild speculation as well as the ethereal idea that we cannot know what heaven is. Now there is purpose and now there is real rest. Now, 1Cor15 becomes a chorus of Hallelujah. The "old chestnut" said that when we die the angel will escourt us to heaven, but never pictured it as anything a human could conceive other than sitting on a cloud with a harp which didn't exactly trill anyone. This book should make your life in Christ complete. The greatest reality of all, we will be with Him who loved us,bought us, taught us, became one of us, included us "in Him" as the Bride, a fantastic home and gives us the privilege of living with and for Him in the completion of His Grand Design. How's those apples?

Glossary of Words and Phrases—Used and Omitted

The phrase "used and omitted" needs explanation. The intent of this book is to communicate meaningful truth in accordance with Scriptural revelation to date. Over almost 2000 years various words and phrases have come to run counter to God's intent and actually communicate nothing of His original intent. Words that when written did distinctly communicate when penned, but have long since failed to do so. Some were a mistranslation from the start and never did hold to the original manuscripts. Some took on the culture in which they first appeared in the English translation. Some have because of so common usage and multiple variations that they have become ethereal. Others by the fact that they have been around so long have become "sacred cows". To the reader it may seem arrogant that an "uncredentialed person as this writer would endeavor to restore credibility to this issue. All I can suggest is that you consider the persons that God used and why he used them. At the end of an era of sophistication, man hinders rather than aids God's purpose.

Words omitted:

1. Church—Where it came from I am not exactly sure. What is sure is that literally it is not even a valid translation. Ekklesia has various meanings, but in the main it is "the called out ones". As such it communicates to the hearer that a selection is being made from some whole at the direction of a person of authority. The doctrine of election now becomes credible and once more an irritant to man. Ekklesia is sometimes plural and sometimes singular. It is not always used exclusively for those groups or persons in the New Testament Era. At the present time a "church" can mean virtually anything man wants it to mean. Its function can be anything man wants it to be to fulfill man's devices. So long as the word "church" is given credibility, peace will exist among ignorant men and it is only when the substance and function is defined that the conflict starts. When religion, not the called out ones, becomes the all incompassing realm, all religions are the same. All have buildings, organizations, . . . etc. The distinction that the human race is dead, blind and under the domination of a person alien to God is lost. Also that God has revealed his plan and will withdraw that which he redeems and discard the rest.The old heaven and earth included. This may seem like a lot of needless verbage, but eminently there is a redeemed group going to be called out and the "Church" will proceed into a lost eternity.

In this book those called out will be referred to as Ephesians conveys, the Body of Christ.

2. Christian— The word appears twice in the New Testament in a history book. It is defined as a "follower of Christ". It is the widest definition and could apply to anyone of any era redeemed by God. It does not in itself communicate much else and in this era can mean what ever one wishes. Some of the greatest scoundrels the world has know were "Christians". The scripture does use the word "brethren" and it in and of its self narrows the scope, but does not apply only to the New Testament. Universally, it is defined as "from the same womb". It appears 629 times in the Old Testament and some 300 times in the New. Given that The Body of Christ, Israel and the Gentiles are separate entities all having a different form of the Gospel, it follows, that the "womb" must be in the existing time and conditions in which the birth took place. Since we no longer at this time have the Gentiles (those before Israel), or Israel as an active entity, it would seem that one who was redeemed in the New Testament, if ask what he is, would reply "a brethren". It communicates the truths of family, having a common parent, a common birth and common destiny as a member of the called out Body of Christ. I don't recall using the word "brethren" in this book other than here, but that's only because it did not come up in the text.

Personal Testimony as a Brethren

Personal comment—Having been "run down"
by the Lord some years ago I spent some time
living in my car on the street, in a friends garage
with his dogs and then in an 8' by 10" room that
had been a cistern. It had a door and window,
both without glass, but some mylar sheets
provided a substitute. I earned my keep by doing
maintenance on the rest of the structure. My
primary task was to go thru the New Testament,
word for word, in Greek. Not having any real
family, I assumed that upon completion of the
task I could attend a existing congregation and
be welcomed by my new family. Wrong! What I
had learned from Scripture had made me even
more weird than before and to say the least it
was perplexing. An old elder appeared and I
shared my plight with him. He sat quietly and
when I finished he had an interesting grin on his
face. "You're a Brethren", he said and that was
the first time I had any knowledge that there
were others that had held to the truth's I had
learned. So with me, I am a Brethren by doctrine
first and I seek fellowship with others on that
same basis.

3. Gospel (the good news)— The word alone, like
   Christian, convey the truth that God will and has
   provided a Christ. Salvation to those of a dead,
   blind, oppressed human race is available. As
   wonderful as redemption is, not all the redeemed
   are brought to the same state and by the same

means. If we were it would defeat God's purpose. In God's creation there are many creations that share large areas of commonality, yet are unique by their differences. Is it so strange then that there are variations of groups of redeemed and a unique form of the gospel to each group.The error that results from assuming that the same gospel is to all in every group makes scripture a confusing mess and a true comprehension of God's plan a impossibility. So "gospel" with no modifier as to its era and grouping communicates little and confuses much. We know little of the gospel to the Gentiles (those prior to Israel). We do know considerable about the Gospel to Israel. The Body of Christ has the Gospel of Grace. The last form of the gospel is to those in the Millennium. With each form come conditions, promises and destinies. Scripture informs us that there would appear in the last days "another gospel" which in truth was not good news in that it was counterfeit. It presents is a reality, so to separate the true from the false the modifier "of Christ" is required in general and 1 of the 4 variations of the true to be specifics.

Preface

Recently while attending a Christian social event, I encountered a gentleman who was very well versed on the Scripture and so we had an enjoyable time reviewing and conversing on that subject. Undoubtedly we saw the revelation of Scripture in a common way. However, that was only true up to a point. That point was Heaven. I ask a series of questions as to the substance, purpose, function and specifics of such a place and it was evident that I had exceeded the scope of his vision as he began to be irritated. That was not my intent or that of the event, so I review the basis of our commonality and ended the discussion on a pleasant and lighter note. Afterward I was confronted with a problem.

The problem was this. Why couldn't he see what I see? Maybe I'm not seeing right! After all, his response after listening to numerous sound Christian men was the norm and mine was not.

The event took place on Saturday night and so on my return home I had my quiet time and I inquired to my Father about the issue. There were no miraculous responses and I retired for the evening.

As is my custom on Sunday morning, I tuned into a well known Bible teacher. The announcer preceded the teacher with this question. "Why do some people in Scripture see and others do not?" The teacher then proceeded to exposit on the Book of Numbers and the account of the 12 spies. It is outside the scope of my intent to recount all the events and their details, but I took it as a Scriptural answer. Israel had come to a point past which they would not advance, even at Jehovah's direction. Only 2 of the 12 saw it God's way and they returned to the Wilderness of Zin. The excuse for such an action was that it was their concern for the children. The dissenters were God's people and He took excellent care of them, but they died in that wilderness. Only the two that saw it God's way and the children progressed to Canaan.

So what has all this to do with Heaven? From all that I've heard in my 73 years, the first few didn't count, you would think the Scriptures are silent on the "what, where, why and who of heaven. That however is not the case, and if men choose to take that position they do so as a matter of choice and not because God has placed some limitation on them. As for me, I chose to see and it is glorious and within the confines of Scripture that has been available for almost 2000 years. Scripture is progressive, so let's not get hung up on some traditional "point". For instance, Reformation Theology has its place in the revelation of God, but it is not the total substance or end of same. He said his Spirit would show us all things, so let's explore the Revelation to the end.

It should be noted that the presentation of Heaven is not all that is new. In the book titled "Major Bible Themes" authored by Chafer/ Walvoord the same basic understanding is presented in the section entitled "The

New Heaven and the New Earth". It's now the best part of 50 years since that concept was authored and a great deal has transpired that provides clarification since that time. Then satellites and space travel were in their infancy. It's no discredit to these authors, they like Pilgrim on his way to the Celestial City saw the pillars and the lions in the way but not the restraints. This book presents a different time sequence, different participants, and a different overall view of the composition and interdependent relationship between the New Jerusalem and Israel in the millennium. It starts with the person of God the designer, his attributes and without wavering from them progresses to completion in reality and function when His design is complete.

Much is made of the Promises that God has made in Scripture to specific people and it's justified. However, misapplication has produced numerous errors and confusion. Failure to pay strict attention to the detail of the who, why, where, when and how of these promises is a dangerous error.

Presented in this book are, in the authors words, two subassemblies. Scripture refers to them differently.

Joh 10:16 And <2532> other <243> sheep <4263> I have <2192> (5719), which <3739> are <2076> (5748) not <3756> of <1537> this <5026> fold <833>: them also <2548> I <3165> must <1163> (5748) bring <71> (5629), and <2532> they shall hear <191> (5692) my <3450> voice <5456>; and <2532> there shall be <1096> (5695) one <3391> fold <4167>, and one <1520> shepherd <4166>.

Our Lord is speaking. He refers to two entities. Those there present, elements of the Nation of Israel, and the other undefined. He does, however, communicate that He will bring both and join them at some point in his design. Remember that for later understanding. Some error at this point, using the Ephesians 2 passage and others to do so.

Eph 2:15 Having abolished <2673> (5660) in <1722> his <846> flesh <4561> the enmity <2189>, even the law <3551> of commandments <1785> contained in <1722> ordinances <1378>; for to <2443> make <2936> (5661) in <1722> himself <1438> of twain <1417> one <1519> <1520> new <2537> man <444>, so making <4160> (5723) peace <1515>;

The error is that Israel is just the precursor of the Body of Christ. The volume of scripture that has to be ignored to assume such a position is considerable. The intent here is not to correct such an error because in a short while reality will settle the issue without human involvement.

There were promises make by God to both entities. They will be fulfilled. Let's look at some examples.

To Israel we have this well know prayer given by God himself. This was instructive to persons present there having only the capacity afforded them according to God's program at that time. No one there met the criteria required for a place or participation in the Body of Christ.

Mt 6:9 after this manner <3779> therefore <3767> pray <4336> (5737) ye <5210>: Our <2257> Father <3962> which <3588> art in <1722> heaven <3772>, Hallowed be <37> (5682) thy <4675> name <3686>.

Mt 6:10 Thy <4675> kingdom <932> come <2064> (5628). Thy <4675> will <2307> be done <1096> (5676) in <1909> earth <1093>, as <2532> <5613> it is in <1722> heaven <3772>.

The prayer is addressed to "Our Father", Plural and corporate, not individual and personal. It speaks of a kingdom that will come on earth as it is in heaven. With the acknowledgement that those with a bias and etheral interpretation have made, no such kingdom has appeared that meets His criteria. It will appear shortly, but not until there are radical changes. The 70th week is required to purify true Israel and fit them for a new heaven and, a new earth.

The above is by no means any recounting of all that is promised to Israel, but it is sufficient to establish that that Nation is and will ever be alive in God's eternal plan.

Given that the reader can't accept the plenary verbal, spiritual, inspired words of our Lord, it is evident that you have a far greater problem than the subject of promises.

What were the promises to the other entity, the Mystery, the Body of Christ? Again, as with Israel, it is not the intent to give a complete listing of these promises to the

Body of Christ, but enough that will establish that they do exist and where they will find their ultimate fulfillment.

Eph 2:4 but <1161> God <2316>, who is <5607> (5752) rich <4145> in <1722> mercy <1656>, for <1223> his <846> great <4183> love <26> wherewith <3739> he loved <25> (5656) us <2248>,

Eph 2:5 even <2532> when we <2248> were <5607> (5752) dead <3498> in sins <3900>, hath quickened us together with <4806> (5656) Christ <5547>, (by grace <5485> ye are <2075> (5748) saved <4982> (5772);)

Eph 2:6 and <2532> hath raised us up together <4891> (5656), and <2532> made us sit together <4776> (5656) in <1722> heavenly <2032> places in <1722> Christ <5547> Jesus <2424>:

For our purpose it is enough to establish our relationship to Christ and our position in eternity. He has quickened us together as a body with Christ, by Grace, not law, raised us up together and made us sit together. Where?, in heavenly places in Christ Jesus. No slave, no servant, but a joint heir, a functional part of the New Man, there to perform those practical tangible task of the Designer. Forget the "harps and clouds and fairy stories. What ever can't readily be understood from this scripture, it is plain that our place is not on earth, but in heavenly places in Him.

The following verse is well known and a common text by those who believe in the "snatching out" of the Body of Christ. That's all well and great, but I would bring to the attention of the reader and ask that they pay special attention to a portion of it that is not commonly emphasized.

1Th 4:17 Then <1899> we <2249> which <3588> are alive <2198> (5723) and remain <4035> (5742) shall be caught up <726> (5691) together <260> with <4862> them <846> in <1722> the clouds <3507>, to <1519> meet <529> the Lord <2962> in <1519> the air <109>: and <2532> so <3779> shall we <2071> <0> ever <3842> be <2071> (5704) with <4862> the Lord <2962>.

It states that we will be caught up to meet the Lord. Where do we meet him?,—in the air. Now pay attention! "and so shall we ever be with the Lord", where?—in the air. For the number of sound expositors that have their eye on choice land in the New Earth, this will not be good news.

All this verbage is required to establish that there are two entities, promised uniquely different things, in different places, to perform specific functions. This knowledge is essential to the text about to be studied.

The major text to be explored is Revelation chapters 21 & 22. Various questions will be answered by these texts and numerous other text. Heaven where? Who and what defines the occupants? What is the larger context in which heaven exists. What function does it serve? But, before we work thru the text, it is necessary to define the terms for sake of narrowing the focus and dispelling numerous misconceptions that have crept in over the years. A clear review of the Architect, his plan, his facility, his process and his ultimate completed project are in view. Every phase will maintain perfectly and in order the intent, character and attributes of the Designer, free from the contamination of man. We will take them in the order of their creation.

The Architect, Plan, Facility, Process & Finished Product

You cannot view heaven as a separate and unrelated entity. It is part of a plan. Even in the plan heaven is different for different elements of the plan. This book pertains to heaven as it pertains to the Body of Christ. In order to rightly track and comprehend the plan as a whole it is necessary to progressively understand each stage, its character and function within the plan. In this plan God is the Architect. If we rightly comprehend the revelation that God has proved of himself, then it follows that every element, in whatever stage it is produced, will have the same character and attributes as those of the Architect. So in progressing thru the stages of the plan, should anything appear that is inconsistent with the character and attributes of the Architect, it would be apparent that it is false. With those thoughts, let's make a journey through the plan. Having done so, we can key on our topic, Heaven as it pertains to the Body of Christ.

God, The Architect

Everything has a source. History shows that man has the aspiration for something comparable to heaven, but he is not the source. Man may have the aspiration, but it is God that put the aspiration in the man. The source of heaven is God's creation. The first aspect of God's revelation to man and that which is commonly taught in Systematic Theology is called Theology Proper. Simply put, it is the revelation of what God has communicated about himself. It is not the purpose of this book to review or teach Theology Proper. It is however, necessary to establish enough knowledge about the character and attributes of the source as it will be required to consistently and accurately monitor the stages of the plan.

A list of attributes about God could be given here, but again it's probably not necessary. A few attributes will be given just to establish what the source is and does.

Initially He reveals He is perfect. Granted I have met a couple persons who labored under this delusion for a while, but alas it was short lived. Imperfection for God is not a possibility.

De 32:4 He is the Rock <06697>, his work <06467> is perfect <08549>: for all his ways <01870> are judgment <04941>: a God <0410> of truth <0530> and without iniquity <05766>, just <06662> and right <03477> is he.

2Sa 22:31 As for God <0410>, his way <01870> is perfect <08549>; the word <0565> of the LORD <03068> is tried <06884> (8803): he is a buckler <04043> to all them that trust <02620> (8802) in him.

If we review both the Old Testament and New, we find that as he is perfect, He demands perfection (perfect gifts, perfect sacrifice, perfect law, men made perfect, be ye perfect and so on). It follows then that the heaven that he makes is perfect in its eternal conception right on to its ultimate function.

Well what if he changes? He states that He changes not.

Mal 3:6 For I am the LORD <03068>, I change <08138> (8804) not; therefore ye sons <01121> of Jacob <03290> are not consumed <03615> (8804).

Maybe he had incomplete knowledge! He states that He is Omniscient. No surprises, changes, additions, subtractions are possible. He is the Alpha and Omega, the Beginning and the end.

Doubtless one could continue thru all the communicable and non-communicable attributes, but if all that was know was the information given above, it is adequate to make the case for Heaven's Source.

The Plan in Eternity

So what about His Plan conceived in eternity. Based on what we have established about the Source, it is possible to just carry that which we have learned about the Source over to the Plan. It's perfect in design, substance, quality, quantity and function. No additions or subtractions, no revisions, no addendums, no spare parts list for high probability part failures and wear. It will be completed perfectly and on schedule as He has purposed. If it isn't we have problems with our Source.

The Facility, Location and Schedule

Now a facility, location and schedule is required. Some place to produce the parts, sub-assemblies to complement each other and ultimately the finished functioning design. There is this 3rd rate planet called earth, but it's a wreck—without form and void. He can however restore a small portion for an initial investment. It's outside the scope of eternity but its made up is such that there is a sun by day and a moon by night, so alas there is the element of time or timing for the schedule. Now it's time to start production. Remember, He is perfect, Omninient and immutable.

We know that after the investment in the small portion a perfect garden was created there and a perfect untested man to reside in the garden. However it didn't stay perfect, as man rebelled against his maker and with a little help of a friend was expelled from the garden and became the progenitor of a dead, blind race of men likened to himself and dominated by his rebel friend.

Eph 2:1 And <2532> you <5209> hath he quickened, who were <5607> (5752) dead <3498> in trespasses <3900> and <2532> sins <266>;

John 10:10 The thief <2812> cometh <2064> (5736) not <3756>, but <1508> for to <2443> steal <2813> (5661), and <2532> to kill <2380> (5661), and <2532> to destroy <622> (5661): I <1473> am come <2064> (5627) that <2443> they might have <2192> (5725) life <2222>, and <2532> that they might have <2192> (5725) it more abundantly <4053>.

Strange offer to men that are alive toward God.

Lu 4:18 The Spirit <4151> of the Lord <2962> is upon <1909> me <1691>, because <1752> he hath anointed <5548> (5656) me <3165> to preach the gospel <2097> (5733) to the poor <4434>; he hath sent <649> (5758) me <3165> to heal <2390> (5664) the brokenhearted <4937> (5772) <2588>, to preach <2784> (5658) deliverance <859> to the captives <164>, and <2532> recovering of sight <309> to the blind <5185>, to set <649> (5658) at <1722> liberty <859> them that are bruised <2352> (5772),

Re 3:17 Because <3754> thou sayest <3004> (5719), <3754> I am <1510> (5748) rich <4145>, and <2532> increased with goods <4147> (5758), and <2532> have <2192> (5719) need <5532> of nothing <3762>; and <2532> knowest <1492> (5758) not <3756> that <3754> thou <4771> art <1488> (5748) wretched <5005>, and <2532> miserable <1652>, and <2532> poor <4434>, and <2532> blind <5185>, and <2532> naked <1131>:

Though the human race was dead, blind and dominated by the adversary, It did provide the source of "raw material" for the progression in Gods plan.

With everything running to plan the redemptive element is introduced into the production process. This redemption at its base would cover the entire production time, however it would take on a character of the segment presently in work. The segments being those prior to Israel, Israel, the Body of Christ and the Millennium. Its function in the period prior to Israel is vague. It was characterized by law during the era of Israel, became the gospel of Grace during the fabrication of the Body of Christ and will in the future function in the Millennium. So why bring this issue up? It is precisely to bring to light that not all redeemed persons will have the same heaven. Israel was promised their heaven on earth.

Lu 11:2 And <1161> he said <2036> (5627) unto them <846>, When <3752> ye pray <4336> (5741), say <3004> (5720), Our <2257> Father <3962> which <3588> art in <1722> heaven <3772>, Hallowed be <37> (5682) thy <4675> name <3686>. Thy <4675> kingdom <932> come <2064> (5628). Thy <4675> will <2307> be done <1096> (5676), as <5613> in <1722> heaven <3772>, so <2532> in <1909> earth <1093>.

Probably one of the greatest error of Bible expositors is the failure to keep, in their entirety, the segment designs of Israel, the Body of Christ and the Millennium separate. Just because they have a common architect and some similarities does not give license to the expositor to co-mingle aspects of a specific segment to another segment. In doing so, man has corrupted God's plan with the excuse that he is aiding it. The inverse is also deplorable. That is simply to ignore the revelation of Scripture and say that everything from Genesis to Revelation is homogeneous.

So the bottom line is that though there are redeemed in every segment, or better described, sub-assembly, and their heaven is not the same. It is not the intent of this book to deal with an earthly people who were promised their Heaven on earth. <u>The intent then is to explore what the Scripture says about Heaven as promised to Body of Christ.</u>

The Final Assembly

The ultimate conclusion then is the final assembly stage where the two sub-assemblies Israel and the Body of Christ) are united to function as a unit (John 17) during the Millennium. As one works thru the Old Testament and the New,it seems that scripture conflicts on many issues. If the segments (sub-assemblies) are maintained as they were designed and joined at this final assemble, the conflicts go away. The reason being that the areas of difference were exclusive to one part or the other. For example, the fact that the New Jerusalem has no temple is not a contradiction with the fact that the Millennium has a temple. It is no longer two entities, but one perfectly harmonized homogeneous unit. The Scriptures in the completed unit complement, not contrast each other. The picture of the New Jerusalem and the New Earth is of one harmonized unit.

The following verse provides the first mark of a parenthesis. Maybe like the first "bookend" in a set is a better way of putting it. The mating "bookend" is found in Rev 22:6. The content of the parenthesis is the phrase "faithful and true".

Re 21:5 And <2532> he that sat <2521> (5740) upon <1909> the throne <2362> said <2036> (5627), Behold <2400> (5628), I make <4160> (5719) all things <3956>

new <2537>. And <2532> he said <3004> (5719) unto me <3427>, Write <1125> (5657): for <3754> these <3778> words <3056> are <1526> (5748) true <228> and <2532> faithful <4103>.

Let's consider the "all things" that are new. He created a new heaven, a new earth, a new Jerusalem, a new man, a new Israel, new commandments, a new covenant and so on. How do they come together and when? Down at the potters shop, He didn't just add wax on the imperfections. He didn't call for reformation the of man, but for a total remake. As to the joining of "all things", we know he won't put "new patches on old wine skins". No, all the new parts come together at the same time at which the unit is perfectly, totally functional. The only time that "fits the bill" to further his program is at the end of the Great Tribulation period. He concludes with:

Rev 22:6 And <2532> he said <2036> (5627) unto me <3427>, It is done <1096> (5754). I <1473> am <1510> (5748) Alpha <1> and <2532> Omega <5598>, the beginning <746> and <2532> the end <5056>. I <1473> will give <1325> (5692) unto him that is athirst <1372> (5723) of <1537> the fountain <4077> of the water <5204> of life <2222> freely <1432>.

Prior to working thru the text, it is probably well to insert an old tool from the past. The Golden rule of Interpretation

When the plain sense of Scripture makes common sense, seek no other sense, therefore, take every word at it's primary, ordinary, usual, literal meaning unless the facts of the immediate context, studied in the light of related passages and axiomatic and fundamental truths, indicate clearly otherwise.

Setting the stage

Where are we in our progression? Relative to time, the sub-assembly known as the Body of Christ is complete. It was perfect in accord with the original design. There would be no additions or alterations. It was unique in respect to that which had preceded it and that which would follow it. Its "lively stones" had been redeemed on the basis that Calvary's work was finished, they were indwelt by the Holy Spirit, gifted and had the Risen Lord functioning as their advocate. Its "school days" were done. It had been removed from the setting in which it had been produced and was ready for the next stage of assembly. That was, however, not true of the first sub-assembly, Israel. From Revelation chapter 4 and most of the rest of the Book of the Revelation, that which we refer to as the Great Tribulation, is executing on earth. Its purpose was to execute the final 70th period in their history and would be the time of purification in preparation of true Israel to enter the millennium era. The millennium is not just an extension of life on a reformed old earth but would be comprised of all the "new" elements that would comprise the finished unit. As the Body of Christ had been created by the uniting of Jew and Gentile to make one new man in the Body of Christ, now the New Jerusalem and occupants would be united to the New Earth with its occupants to comprise God's finished, unified functional design. No new patches on old wineskins. A new environment (heaven and earth), a new gospel, a new man (bride and bridegroom) a new Jerusalem and a new standard operating procedure both in the New Jerusalem and in the New Earth. So let's begin with Revelation Chapter 21.

P.S. Consentrate on the fact that from here to the end of the book the people being addressed are not the Body of Christ. The revelation of the Bride is contained in the text, but she is already in the New Jerusalem. She is no longer the Body of Christ, but the Bride of Christ and has free access to all the features therein.

Revelation, Chapter 21

John was in extraordinary circumstances, but he was very much a common man as we are. He "called it as he saw it" and described what he saw in reference to that which he had been exposed in everyday life.

Rev21:1 And <2532> I saw <1492> (5627) a new <2537> heaven <3772> and <2532> a new <2537> earth <1093>: for <1063> the first <4413> heaven <3772> and <2532> the first <4413> earth <1093> were passed away <3928> (5627); and <2532> there was <2076> (5748) no <3756> more <2089> sea <2281>.

John simply states the fact of what he saw. What he saw was different in its makeup than the heaven and earth he was used to. What he was used to was under his feet with its familiar features but what he saw was before his eyes. Probably the most outstanding difference was easily visible as there was no sea. It is worthy to note that what he saw was not the product of man and did exist.

The feature of the sea alone raises numerous questions. Is the moon required now that there is no sea? No sea, so there are no tides. It is note worthy to remember that the irony of Noah's Ark was that there wasn't rain or a body of water in existence. So its not like the condition had not existed before. According to Rev. 21:23, there is no moon in the New Jerusalem. So where is the New Jerusalem? The sea (salt water) is a cathartic for cleansing the water system on the old earth, but with the ideal conditions of the new earth it is no longer required. We are used to viewing earth and seeing blue, but having said nothing of anything else being changed, green becomes the most likely prominent color for the New Earth. Given that the size of earth remains constant, the land mass is greatly increased. This has brought some to speculate that the number of persons to be redeemed in an ideal condition would dwarf the number redeemed in the first earth. What we do know for certain is, this isn't the first time the issue of a new heaven and earth has come up.

Peter foresaw something of the same revelation. The era was the "day of God".

2Pet 3:12 Looking for <4328> (5723) and <2532> hasting <4692> (5723) unto the coming <3952> of the day <2250> of God <2316>, wherein <1223> <3739> the heavens <3772> being on fire <4448> (5746) shall be dissolved <3089> (5701), and <2532> the elements <4747> shall melt <5080> (5743) with fervent heat <2741> (5746)?

The actors and activity in this verse are the spirits of devils working miracles, impressing the kings of the earth and the world to rally them to battle on that great day of God Almighty. Peter adds that in the course of such an action the heavens being on fire shall be dissolved and the elements shall melt from the heat. This would seem to shed light on the "passing away" of the old heaven and earth prior to the millennium.

2 Pet 3: 13 Nevertheless <1161> we <4328> <0>, according to <2596> his <846> promise <1862>, look for <4328> (5719) new <2537> heavens <3772> and <2532> a new <2537> earth <1093>, wherein <1722> <3739> dwelleth <2730> (5719) righteousness <1343>.

Malachi gives us this.

Mal 4:1 For behold, the day <03117> cometh <0935> (8802), that shall burn <01197> (8802) as an oven <08574>; and all the proud <02086>, yea, and all that do <06213> (8802) wickedly <07564>, shall be stubble <07179>: and the day <03117> that cometh <0935> (8802) shall burn them up <03857> (8765), saith <0559> (8804) the LORD <03068> of hosts <06635>, that it shall leave <05800> (8799) them neither root <08328> nor branch <06057>.

In the Old Testament, Isaiah makes a similar reference.

Isaiah 65:17 For, behold, I create <01254> (8802) new <02319> heavens <08064> and a new <02319> earth <0776>: and the former <07223> shall not be remembered <02142> (8735), nor come <05927> (8799) into mind <03820>.

So in addition to what we have learned from Revelation, we now know that the "out with the old and in with the new" is absolute. The question is often ask, "Will we remember what went on in the old earthly existence?". If there is a scriptural answer, this verse would seem to apply. It won't even reside in the mind. Again, this could have relation to the Lord's teaching that you don't put new patches on old wine skins. Remembering the old would seem to serve the fleshly emotions, but not God's eternal intent. The new is exclusively NEW!

Continuing with Isaiah: (Note that in the case of Israel some things are preserved)

Isa. 66:22 For as the new <02319> heavens <08064> and the new <02319> earth <0776>, which I will make <06213> (8802), shall remain <05975> (8802) before <06440> me, saith <05002> (8803) the LORD <03068>, so shall your seed <02233> and your name <08034> remain <05975> (8799).

Though the Hebrew language is used, the word "new" retains the same character as in the New Testament. In both verses the text is to Israel. Now we see that when this new heaven and new earth are created, the relationship of the LORD and Israel remains. Israel is still before the LORD, but as we shall see, the proximity has changed. What we have yet to establish is where God is when he brings this to pass.

Sensationalism is not the objective here, but with man's advanced capability to observe the heavens and the universe in which this heaven and earth abide, it might be well to note that which seems to be coming or is the everyday information as to other bodies similar to our earth. How do you "swap out" a heaven and an earth? For that matter, how did He speak ours into existence? Genesis tells us that our earth was "without form and void". Modern science tells us numerous such bodies presently exist in such a state. The latest pictures of such entities from the Hubbell Telescope are indeed spectacular and to say the least awesome. However, it's doubtful that you'd want to live there now or for eternity without a few improvements. For those that lived in the 1940s and upward, Scriptural concepts as are positively stated here were outside the acceptable realm or possibility. Now such Scriptural concepts are acceptable, not only to Bible Students, but to the lost world. Granted the particulars on how this will come about varies greatly.

Rev21: 2 And <2532> I <1473> John <2491> saw <1492> (5627) the holy <40> city <4172>, new <2537> Jerusalem <2419>, coming down <2597> (5723) from <575> God <2316> out of <1537> heaven <3772>, prepared <2090> (5772) as <5613> a bride <3565> adorned <2885> (5772) for her <846> husband <435>.

John continues observing. Like him then, and us now, some men see and some don't. Without the substance of revelation, the illumination of the Spirit and an enabled receiver, there remains just wild speculation in darkness. Heaven is no "speculation in darkness" to those with eyes to see. Sadly this pertains not just to Israel, but to the body of Christ. Our Lord spoke of same in the Mystery Parables:

Mt 13:15 For <1063> this <5127> people's <2992> heart <2588> is waxed gross <3975> (5681), and <2532> their ears <3775> are dull <917> of hearing <191> (5656), and <2532> their <846> eyes <3788> they have closed <2576> (5656); lest at any time <3379> they should see <1492> (5632) with their eyes <3788>, and <2532> hear

<191> (5661) with their ears <3775>, and <2532> should understand <4920> (5632) with their heart <2588>, and <2532> should be converted <1994> (5661), and <2532> I should heal <2390> (5667) them <846>

The present malignity of the Body of Christ is "sleep and slumber". Peter speaks of this as "spiritual blindness". It's a sad reality.

2Pe 1:8 For <1063> if these things <5023> be <5225> (5723) in you <5213>, and <2532> abound <4121> (5723), they make <2525> (5719) you that ye shall neither <3756> be barren <692> nor <3761> unfruitful <175> in <1519> the knowledge <1922> of our <2257> Lord <2962> Jesus <2424> Christ <5547>.

2Pe 1:9 But <1063> he that <3739> lacketh <3361> <3918> (5748) these things <5023> is <2076> (5748) blind <5185>, and cannot see afar off <3467> (5723), and hath forgotten <3024> <2983> (5631) that he was purged from <2512> his <846> old <3819> sins <266>.

The other side of this issue is also addressed.

Mt 13:16 But <1161> blessed <3107> are your <5216> eyes <3788>, for <3754> they see <991> (5719): and <2532> your <5216> ears <3775>, for <3754> they hear <191> (5719).

What was the substance of the revelation? It was not just a city, but a holy city. Doubtless it didn't have a sign on it, "holy city", so John's Illumination and enablement are functioning. If we remember the holiness of our

Source, the revelator (the Holy Spirit), the description of the city should be no surprise. The city is in accord with the word "holy" and is both set apart and characterized by its Source. The fact that it is "set apart" differentiates it from the old Jerusalem which was an integral part of the physical earth and was not a closed city as is the New Jerusalem. Old Jerusalem's central geographical location was by design in the earth and its holiness was God's intent, but that's not how it turned out. The position of the New Jerusalem is interesting. At Calvary our Lord was suspended between heaven and earth, so it is interesting that in the millennium his home and position relative to the New Earth is also suspended between heaven and earth.

God is holy and holiness is not optional. One of the sad realities of our day is that a false evangelism is prevalent that feeds the flesh and forgets holiness altogether. Any God fearing person living in our present condition will get a fore boding feeling every time the holiness issue is raised.

1Pe 1:16 Because <1360> it is written <1125> (5769), Be ye <1096> (5634) holy <40>; for <3754> I <1473> am <1510> (5748) holy <40>.

It is important to note not only the nature of the city, but the fact that it is indeed a city. What John saw was something he was very familiar with as a concept of a city went, however what he was familiar with was anything but holy. People lived and functioned in the city he saw. If the construction material is as stated, they would be visible.

The phrase "the holy city" in reference to Jerusalem does appear in the Old Testament. Some verses are included for your consideration.

Ne 11:1 And the rulers <08269> of the people <05971> dwelt <03427> (8799) at Jerusalem <03389>: the rest <07605> of the people <05971> also cast <05307> (8689) lots <01486>, to bring <0935> (8687) one <0259> of ten <06235> to dwell <03427> (8800) in Jerusalem <03389> the holy <06944> city <05892>, and nine <08672> parts <03027> to dwell in other cities <05892>.

Ne 11:18 All the Levites <03881> in the holy <06944> city <05892> were two hundred <03967> fourscore <08084> and four <0702>.

Isa 48:2 For they call <07121> (8738) themselves of the holy <06944> city <05892>, and stay <05564> (8738) themselves upon the God <0430> of Israel <03478>; The LORD <03068> of hosts <06635> is his name <08034>.

It is evident that the "holy city" in the previous verses was on the old earth.

The next verse is of particular interest as it pertains to Zion and Jerusalem. Like the phrase, "unto us a child is born, unto us a son is given" the interlude in time and the relative positions between the two elements is of considerable importance.

Isa 52:1 Awake <05782> (8798), awake <05782> (8798); put on <03847> (8798) thy strength <05797>, O Zion <06726>; put on <03847> (8798) thy beautiful <08597>

garments <0899>, O Jerusalem <03389>, the holy <06944> city <05892>: for henceforth there shall no more <03254> (8686) come <0935> (8799) into thee the uncircumcised <06189> and the unclean <02931>.

There is a Mount Zion and a city of Jerusalem today. However when the old heaven and earth pass away, they go too. Zionism is more than just a place, it is a concept. No doubt it continues. The description of Jerusalem as given here is interesting in that it is a closed city. Jerusalem on the earth was not a closed city, but the New Jerusalem is a closed city as our text will soon reveal. So the period of application of this verse would tend to be in the New Creation.

The New Jerusalem was a functional city with all those features one would expect to find in any city. Granted, it was different indeed as our word "new" informs us again, but it was recognizable as something common to men as a functioning city. Again we are not speculating. Scriptural data and dimensions which follow eliminate that possibility.

John informs us that the city has a name, the New Jerusalem. He was well familiar with the old one. It still existed and though the New Jerusalem appeared, the old one didn't disappear at this point in time. They were, however separate. It was said to descend, so given John's position on the existing earth, its movement was from some distance relative to his position to a position closer to his position. Let's be clear here about what is said and what is not. He did not state that it descended to the old earth. If it had or should in the future the aspect of holiness would have been corrupted as surely as mixing the concept of Law with Grace. As will later be stated, corruption has no part in the New Jerusalem. Granted at this point the separation of the New Jerusalem and the New earth is still not fully established.

John tells us that this New Jerusalem is a prepared place. The word speaks of the advance preparations commonly made for a prominent person. It says, "as a bride adorned". So who's got a wife and who's got a bride? Jehovah spoke of Israel as his wife. So who is the bride for?

Now we touch the "holy grail" of heaven.

Joh 14:1 Let <5015> <0> not <3361> your <5216> heart <2588> be troubled <5015> (5744): ye believe <4100> (5719) (5720) in <1519> God <2316>, believe <4100> (5719) (5720) also <2532> in <1519> me <1691>.

Joh 14:2 In <1722> my <3450> Father's <3962> house <3614> are <1526> (5748) many <4183> mansions <3438>: if it were not <1490> so, I would have told <302> <2036> (5627) you <5213>. I go <4198> (5736) to prepare <2090> (5658) a place <5117> for you <5213>.

Joh 14:3 And <2532> if <1437> I go <4198> (5680) and <2532> prepare <2090> (5661) a place <5117> for you <5213>, I will come <2064> (5736) again <3825>, and <2532> receive <3880> (5695) you <5209> unto <4314> myself <1683>; that <2443> where <3699> I <1473> am <1510> (5748), there ye <5210> may be <5600> (5753) also <2532>.

Joh 14:4 And <2532> whither <3699> I <1473> go <5217> (5719) ye know <1492> (5758), and <2532> the way <3598> ye know <1492> (5758).

With the full realization that some will be offended, I shall proceed to offend. At this point in time there was no human in the room constituted to be qualified as part of the Body of Christ. They were not personally redeemed by His shed Blood, indwelt by the Holy Spirit, Gifted and with a personal Advocate seated at the right hand of God. Our Lord spoke in the "eternal now" with the full knowledge that what God had conceived in eternity was fully accomplished. The persons to whom he spoke were at best a choir of questions with no more capacity or capability to comprehend Him at that time than the natural man of that day. Some were candidates elect for the Body of Christ. Every person in the room had only one mode of redemption at that specific time and that was with a Covenant Nation and a gospel of law. It's not as though He would not fulfill every aspect of that which he had promised to Israel. The promises did include a place for His covenant people in His eternal plan, but it was not in heaven. Again they were promised, "thy kingdom come, on earth <u>as it is in heaven</u>".

All that to say that He went and prepared a place for his Bride not yet in existence. He wasn't addressing Israel corporate. In the future, in time, the Body of Christ would be conceived, prepared and those who constitute its makeup would have a full knowledge of the past, present and future. He repeatedly told his disciples to ask for the Spirit, but in the end He had to do it for them.

Joh 14:26 But <1161> the Comforter <3875>, which is the Holy <40> Ghost <4151>, whom <3739> the Father <3962> will send <3992> (5692) in <1722> my <3450> name <3686>, he <1565> shall teach <1321> (5692) you <5209> all things <3956>, and <2532> bring <5279> <0> all things <3956> to <5279> <0> your <5209> remembrance <5279> (5692), whatsoever <3739> I have said <2036> (5627) unto you <5213>.

It is however those described as the Bride, and they only, which shall share in as joint heirs in Christ in the New Jerusalem.

The Apostle Paul speaks of such a preparation.

2Co 11:2 For <1063> I am jealous <2206> (5719) over you <5209> with godly <2316> jealousy <2205>: for <1063> I have espoused <718> (5668) you <5209> to one <1520> husband <435>, that I may present <3936> (5658) you as a chaste <53> virgin <3933> to Christ <5547>.

I would hope the reader is familiar with the Scripture relative to the construction of the Body of Christ (Eph.) and the Head (Col.) coming together to make the new man. He stated He is creating all things new and this element is one of seven in the total project. The Body of Christ as the Bride and the Lord Jesus as the Bridegroom is amply evident. What is being established here is where the new man will reside and what will he be doing after the construction of the marriage has transpired.

Rev21:3 And <2532> I heard <191> (5656) a great <3173> voice <5456> out of <1537> heaven <3772> saying

<3004> (5723), Behold <2400> (5628), the tabernacle <4633> of God <2316> is with <3326> men <444>, and <2532> he will dwell <4637> (5692) with <3326> them <846>, and <2532> they <846> shall be <2071> (5704) his <846> people <2992>, and <2532> God <2316> himself <846> shall be <2071> (5704) with <3326> them <846>, and be their <846> God <2316>.

John hears a great voice. Scripture refers to the phrase "great voice" in the following verses. If reviewed the identity of the speaker is established.

The Lord from Sinai—De 5:22 These words <01697> the LORD <03068> spake <01696> (8765) unto all your assembly <06951> in the mount <02022> out of the midst <08432> of the fire <0784>, of the cloud <06051>, and of the thick darkness <06205>, with a great <01419> voice <06963>: and he added no more <03254> (8804). And he wrote <03789> (8799) them in two <08147> tables <03871> of stone <068>, and delivered <05414> (8799) them unto me.

Judgement of Bablylon—Jer 51:55 Because the LORD <03068> hath spoiled <07703> (8802) Babylon <0894>, and destroyed <06> (8765) out of her the great <01419> voice <06963>; when her waves <01530> do roar <01993> (8804) like great <07227> waters <04325>, a noise <07588> of their voice <06963> is uttered <05414> (8738):

John (pre-Tribulation)—Re 1:10 I was <1096> (5633) in <1722> the Spirit <4151> on <1722> the Lord's <2960> day <2250>, and <2532> heard <191> (5656) behind

<3694> me <3450> a great <3173> voice <5456>, as <5613> of a trumpet <4536>,

The restoring & ascension of 2 witnesses—Re 11:12 And <2532> they heard <191> (5656) a great <3173> voice <5456> from <1537> heaven <3772> saying <3004> (5723) unto them <846>, Come up <305> (5628) hither <5602>. And <2532> they ascended up <305> (5627) to <1519> heaven <3772> in <1722> a cloud <3507>; and <2532> their <846> enemies <2190> beheld <2334> (5656) them <846>.

God commanding angels, vials on earth—Re 16:1 And <2532> I heard <191> (5656) a great <3173> voice <5456> out of <1537> the temple <3485> saying <3004> (5723) to the seven <2033> angels <32>, Go your ways <5217> (5720), and <2532> pour out <1632> (5657) the vials <5357> of the wrath <2372> of God <2316> upon <1519> the earth <1093>.

God commanding 7th angel, vial on air—Re 16:17 And <2532> the seventh <1442> angel <32> poured out <1632> (5656) his <846> vial <5357> into <1519> the air <109>; and <2532> there came <1831> (5627) a great <3173> voice <5456> out of <575> the temple <3485> of heaven <3772>, from <575> the throne <2362>, saying <3004> (5723), It is done <1096> (5754).

Much people in heaven glorifying—Re 19:1 And <2532> after <3326> these things <5023> I heard <191> (5656) a great <3173> voice <5456> of much <4183> people <3793> in <1722> heaven <3772>, saying <3004> (5723), Alleluia <239>; Salvation <4991>, and <2532> glory

<1391>, and <2532> honour <5092>, and <2532> power <1411>, unto the Lord <2962> our <2257> God <2316>:

John conveys the message of the voice. The Tribulation is over and the purification being complete, God now establishes the new condition. Much like the need for the just clearing of sin prior to the operation of Grace, God will Himself establish the new conditions of His finished design.

Behold!, or in Americana," WOW!, take a look at this". The Tabernacle, not the replica that Moses built, is with men (plural). And He will dwell with them. If one considers what went on in the earthly tabernacle and what is being stated here, dwelling with men, it really magnifies the word "new" beyond description. Not since the first Adam have we seen such a relationship, but now it's with "them". And they shall be His people. No more separation, rejections, divorce and condemnation, they are truly his people. Hosea must be jumping up and down! And God himself will be with them. No SHEKINA Glory secluded in the Holy of Holies, but total access. Kind of sounds like Romans 5 and that which had been the condition and intent in the Garden was now a reality, not for some but for all.

God erases the darkness of sin:

Rev21:4 And <2532> God <2316> shall wipe away <1813> (5692) all <3956> tears <1144> from <575> their <846> eyes <3788>; and <2532> there shall be <2071> (5704) no <3756> more <2089> death <2288>, neither <3777> sorrow <3997>, nor <3777> crying <2906>,

42

neither <3777> <3756> shall there be <2071> (5704) any more <2089> pain <4192>: for <3754> the former things <4413> are passed away <565> (5627).

The source of the human anguish, pain, heartache, quandary, all gone! To expound this account would be impossible. To rejoice in its absence is heaven.

Rev21:5 And <2532> he that sat <2521> (5740) upon <1909> the throne <2362> said <2036> (5627), Behold <2400> (5628), I make <4160> (5719) all things <3956> new <2537>. And <2532> he said <3004> (5719) unto me <3427>, Write <1125> (5657): for <3754> these <3778> words <3056> are <1526> (5748) true <228> and <2532> faithful <4103>.

John not only sees a throne which our text will clarify later, but a person seated on that throne. Who is the person? In general, it is God, but which person of the Godhead? If we take what has been presented and discard that which is not, the person is the Lamb, the Lord Jesus.

He states that "I make all things new". It is a tangible work in progress and its composition is new. He commands John to create a written record and declares it to be faithful and true. The record would ultimately provide instruction to not only the Body of Christ, but to those to who it would most directly apply.

In the Old Testament, when the human family was utterly corrupt, it was suggested to God that He simply "start over". However, there were, unknown to man, "mysteries" yet to be built and God never deviated from his design. He was always "setting his face toward the objective". Now, "it is done", there is nothing left but to record the accomplishments and identify the Designer. Our Lord Jesus, the Christ said in reference to the work of salvation, "It is finished". Now relative to the Plan of the Ages, He declares,"It is done".

Rev21: 6 And <2532> he said <2036> (5627) unto me <3427>, It is done <1096> (5754). I <1473> am <1510> (5748) Alpha <1> and <2532> Omega <5598>, the beginning <746> and <2532> the end <5056>.

I <1473> will give <1325> (5692) unto him that is athirst <1372> (5723) of <1537> the fountain <4077> of the water <5204> of life <2222> freely <1432>.

What had begun with Him in Eternity and was destine to end in the same place. With all things "new" He was righteously and justly able to extend to his created beings that for which he had previously prepared for them in an unrestricted condition.

Now God divides the spoils, to those who have like "the deer panting for the water" longed for their fulfillment with him and to those that did not, the condition of their chosen end. Justice reigns!

Rev21: 7 He that overcometh <3528> (5723) shall inherit <2816> (5692) all things <3956>; and <2532> I will be <2071> (5704) his <846> God <2316>, and <2532> he <846> shall be <2071> (5704) my <3427> son <5207>.

Unlike those in the Body of Christ whose inheritance is established by Christ himself, those addressed here obtain their inheritance on the basis of overcoming. This is reasonable considering who we are dealing with. What "overcoming" amounts to is somewhat vague. It would appear that a profound temple life and practice is required for those born in the Millennium. How they proceed from being a lost man to having access to the Tree of Life,the Water of Life and sonship with God is unspecified.

The position of son is noteworthy. It is not the word Scripture uses of a child, but a mature, full grown offspring. In this context His son would be in accordance with Israel and not identical with that of the New Testament son.

The New Testament Son would have traveled the Roman Road, understanding man in his original state and that after the fall. He could define the elements of the lost race and relate God's just decree against same. God's justification is his lot. At Calvary, he has observed and experienced the reversal of every element of the Fall in Genesis. The old nature, the law and self have been replaced with a new nature with Grace and Christ at his center. In Romans 8 he is first referred to as Huios, the mature son, ready to be informed of his Father's prior undertakings. He is not a slave, God doesn't make those, or even servant, but joint heir, capable of being an integral functioning element in God's heaven, a joint heir.

The Son spoken of here would be fully in tune with all the history, tradition, ritual and Scripture that pertains to Israel. We have nothing in Scripture to say that in his redemption he is indwelt with the Holy Spirit, gifted or that the Lord Jesus is his personal advocate.

Rev21:8 But <1161> the fearful <1169>, and <2532> unbelieving <571>, and <2532> the abominable <948> (5772), and <2532> murderers <5406>, and <2532> whoremongers <4205>, and <2532> sorcerers <5332>, and <2532> idolaters <1496>, and <2532> all <3956> liars <5571>, shall have their <846> part <3313> in <1722> the lake <3041> which <3588> burneth <2545> (5746) with fire <4442> and <2532> brimstone <2303>: which is <3603> (5748) the second <1208> death <2288>.

The reality of sin in the Millennium holds forth the reality of swift accountability. Where as on the old earth there was prolonged time period between the offence and punishment, in the Millennium that will not be the case. Punishment will be immediate.

John is now approached by the last angel involved in Israel's purification process and directs him to a more precise view of the The New Jerusalem and more specifically the Bride. As C. S. Lewis put it, "further in and further up".

Rev 21: 9 And <2532> there came <2064> (5627) unto <4314> me <3165> one of <1520> the seven <2033> angels <32> which <3588> had <2192> (5723) the seven <2033> vials <5357> full <1073> (5723) of the seven <2033> last <2078> plagues <4127>, and <2532> talked <2980> (5656) with <3326> me <1700>, saying <3004> (5723), Come hither <1204> (5773), I will shew <1166>

(5692) thee <4671> the bride <3565>, the Lamb's <721> wife <1135>.

Previously John saw the New Jerusalem descending prepared as a bride for her husband. Now we get additional information. We are going to see the bride. So since she is visible, it is safe to conclude that she is already abiding there in God's view. So the Bride and the Lamb's wife are one and the same. It states that she is the Lamb's wife. If wife is the proper translation, it is very important because the wedding has already taken place, but where and when? We have to back up for a moment and identify the Bride and the Lamb. We'll take the Lamb first. John the Baptist can help us with that.

Joh 1:36 And <2532> looking upon <1689> (5660) Jesus <2424> as he walked <4043> (5723), he saith <3004> (5719), Behold <2396> the Lamb <286> of God <2316>!

In the New Testament "the Lamb" is used 28 times. As it is not the intent here to explore every verse, only one will be given for our purpose. It contains some familiar phrases that we have already seen in the finished design.

Re 7:17 For <3754> the Lamb <721> which <3588> is in the midst <303> <3319> of the throne <2362> shall feed <4165> (5692) them <846>, and <2532> shall lead <3594> (5692) them <846> unto <1909> living <2198> (5723) fountains <4077> of waters <5204>: and <2532> God <2316> shall wipe away <1813> (5692) all <3956> tears <1144> from <575> their <846> eyes <3788>.

It's safe to say that the Lord Jesus, the lamb of God is the wife's husband. Now we need to link this bride and this husband.

2Co 11:2 For <1063> I am jealous <2206> (5719) over you <5209> with godly <2316> jealousy <2205>: for <1063> I have espoused <718> (5668) you <5209> to one <1520> husband <435>, that I may present <3936> (5658) you as a chaste <53> virgin <3933> to Christ <5547>.

So that being the case, we have the bride, the Lamb's wife, the Body of Christ and the husband, the Lamb of God, the Lord and Christ the Head abiding in the New Jerusalem.

Rev 21:10 And <2532> he carried <667> <0> me <3165> away <667> (5656) in <1722> the spirit <4151> to <1909> a great <3173> and <2532> high <5308> mountain <3735>, and <2532> shewed <1166> (5656) me <3427> that great <3173> city <4172>, the holy <40> Jerusalem <2419>, descending <2597> (5723) out of <1537> heaven <3772> from <575> God <2316>,

Whether bodily or otherwise, John's person was transported to a position of greatest advantage in viewing.

He is "in the spirit". This should be no surprise because he must be compatible with that which he will see. Initially when created, man was primarily spirit, but as a result of his rebellion his spiritual compatibility with his creator was lost.

Joh 4:24 God <2316> is a Spirit <4151>: and <2532> they that worship <4352> (5723) him <846> must <1163> (5748) worship <4352> (5721) him in <1722> spirit <4151> and <2532> in truth <225>.

So John is taken to the top of a mountain for a closer look. It would be strange indeed if he did so to look down to the earth. It would seem that if the New Jerusalem is descending and John is ascending that a closer look would indeed be possible. No need to push the point at the moment.

Once again, as in verse 2, he see that Great City, the New Jerusalem descending out of heaven from God.

In His work at Calvary, he was suspended between heaven and earth. He made a show openly during his work of salvation. Now in His work during the Millennium he is once again suspended between heaven and earth in the New Jerusalem where again he will be visible openly.

The Lighting

Rev 21:11 Having <2192> (5723) the glory <1391> of God <2316>: and <2532> her <846> light <5458> was like <3664> unto a stone <3037> most precious <5093>, even like <5613> a jasper <2393> stone <3037>, clear as crystal <2929> (5723);

So what happened to the Glory of God? Maybe we just found it. It is interesting to note that the phrase "the Glory of God" only has 2 references in the Old Testament.

The New Testament has numerous references, but these three best make the case.

Stephen at his stoning—Ac 7:55 But <1161> he, being <5225> (5723) full <4134> of the Holy <40> Ghost <4151>, looked up stedfastly <816> (5660) into <1519> heaven <3772>, and saw <1492> (5627) the glory <1391> of God <2316>, and <2532> Jesus <2424> standing <2476> (5761) on <1537> the right hand <1188> of God <2316>,

Php 2:11 And <2532> that every <3956> tongue <1100> should confess <1843> (5672) that <3754> Jesus <2424> Christ <5547> is Lord <2962>, to <1519> the glory <1391> of God <2316> the Father <3962>.

Re 21:23 And <2532> the city <4172> had <2192> (5719) no <3756> need <5532> of the sun <2246>, neither <3761> of the moon <4582>, to <2443> shine <5316> (5725) in <1722> it <846>: for <1063> the glory <1391> of God <2316> did lighten <5461> (5656) it <846>, and <2532> the Lamb <721> is the light <3088> thereof <846>.

Where the Lord Jesus is, the glory of God is.

What about "her light"? Light was among the various areas of technology that the author attempted to master. It was short lived. If you can grasp that "God is Light", you'll understand. However, I did learn a little of the angle of incidence and angle of refraction. Simply put, it is what makes gemstones sparkle. The light gets in and can't get out. Imagine a gemstone that is 1500 miles long on each side. Now illuminate it inside with "I am the light of the world". The phrase "Even as a jasper stone" creates some what of a problem in light of the next description, "clear as crystal". Jasper stones are anything but clear, but maybe it is referring to the shape and not the opaque quality. Our city is however crystal clear for reasons which will be given later.

Presently the sun provides the light to the earth and moon the light by night. We will find that the Son replaces the sun. "I am the light of the world" takes on a tangible reality. More on that will come later.

Now to the construction of the city

and its various features

Rev 21:12 And <5037> had <2192> (5723) a wall <5038> great <3173> and <2532> high <5308>, and had <2192> (5723) twelve <1427> gates <4440>, and <2532> at <1909> the gates <4440> twelve <1427> angels <32>, and <2532> names <3686> written thereon <1924> (5772), which <3739> are <2076> (5748) the names of the twelve <1427> tribes <5443> of the children of Israel.

How does a wall 1500mi long and 1500mi high and having a perimeter of 6000mi sound. Great enough. Crystal clear! The sides of many of our modern buildings are almost totally glass. They sparkle in the sunlight. That is nothing compared with this. Here the Son light comes from within as it does in our light bulbs. There is another ornate feature, but we will see that later.

Now to the 12 gates in the wall which are reminiscent of the garden of Eden as there is an angel without each gate. The angels don't have access to the city, but serve as security guards to grant access to those seeking to enter the city. This would be consistent with their function relative to the Body of Christ on the old earth. Much to the dismay of many Bible Scholars, they (angels) have no involvement within the Body of Christ. Involvement Scripturally with candidates for salvation, yes. Involvement with the redeemed in Christ, No. The only gates of importance with the Body of Christ had to do with body parts, but gates played a big part in Israel and as they do here.

Rev 21:13 On <575> the east <395> three <5140> gates <4440>; on <575> the north <1005> three <5140> gates <4440>; on <575> the south <3558> three <5140> gates <4440>; and <2532> on <575> the west <1424> three <5140> gates <4440>.

How Ezekiel saw it: 48:31 And the gates <08179> of the city <05892> shall be after the names <08034> of the tribes <07626> of Israel <03478>: three <07969> gates <08179> northward <06828>; one <0259> gate <08179> of Reuben <07205>, one <0259> gate <08179> of Judah <03063>, one <0259> gate <08179> of Levi <03878>.

Eze48:32 And at the east <06921> side <06285> four <0702> thousand <0505> and five <02568> hundred <03967>: and three <07969> gates <08179>; and one

<0259> gate <08179> of Joseph <03130>, one <0259> gate <08179> of Benjamin <01144>, one <0259> gate <08179> of Dan <01835>.

Eze48:33 And at the south <05045> side <06285> four <0702> thousand <0505> and five <02568> hundred <03967> measures <04060>: and three <07969> gates <08179>; one <0259> gate <08179> of Simeon <08095>, one <0259> gate <08179> of Issachar <03485>, one <0259> gate <08179> of Zebulun <02074>.

Eze48:34 At the west <03220> side <06285> four <0702> thousand <0505> and five <02568> hundred <03967>, with their three <07969> gates <08179>; one <0259> gate <08179> of Gad <01410>, one <0259> gate <08179> of Asher <0836>, one <0259> gate <08179> of Naphtali <05321>.

Eze48:35 It was round about <05439> eighteen <08083> <06240> thousand <0505> measures: and the name <08034> of the city <05892> from that day <03117> shall be, The LORD is there <03074>.

So it should not be conjecture as to who will enter at what gate. The qualifications for entry will follow later. It is also evident who the gate is for.

Rev21:14 And <2532> the wall <5038> of the city <4172> had <2192> (5723) twelve <1427> foundations <2310>, and <2532> in <1722> them <846> the names <3686> of the twelve <1427> apostles <652> of the Lamb <721>.

The exterior of the structure has been described and now we go to the interior. Whatever may be the particulars, these foundations are what we refer to a floors. This is basically a 12 story building. Each floor has an identity and each name is associated exclusively with the New Man.

Rev21:15 And <2532> he that talked <2980> (5723) with <3326> me <1700> had <2192> (5707) a golden <5552> reed <2563> to <2443> measure <3354> (5661) the city <4172>, and <2532> the gates <4440> thereof <846>, and <2532> the wall <5038> thereof <846>.

It leaves the realm of fantasy and speculation when God give hard dimensions and shapes. Did you ever hear or see a city on earth that was foursquare? Cities are generally described as two dimensional. Here we have a 3 dimensional structure.

Rev21:16 And <2532> the city <4172> lieth <2749> (5736) foursquare <5068>, and <2532> the length <3372> <846> is <2076> (5748) as large <5118> as <3745> <2532> the breadth <4114>: and <2532> he measured <3354> (5656) the city <4172> with the reed <2563> <1909>, twelve <1427> thousand <5505> furlongs <4712>. The length <3372> and <2532> the breadth <4114> and <2532> the height <5311> of it <846> are <2076> (5748) equal <2470>. The is about 1500 miles per side.

Rev21:17 And <2532> he measured <3354> (5656) the wall <5038> thereof <846>, an hundred <1540> and forty <5062> and four <5064> cubits <4083>, according to the measure <3358> of a man <444>, that is <3603> (5748), of the angel <32>.

The feature of the wall as it is described is undefined other than to say that it is 216 feet. That probably is the height or width. Maybe John relates back to something that was common in the walls of his day. In Babylon, it is said that the wall was wide enough for a 3 lane road on top and functioned as living quarters. Rahab the Harlot and the spies come to mind in this respect.

Rev21:18 And <2532> the building <1739> of the wall <5038> of it <846> was <2258> (5713) of jasper <2393>: and <2532> the city <4172> was pure <2513> gold <5553>, like <3664> unto clear <2513> glass <5194>.

As a literalist this would seem to produce a problem. However, if one travels to a city in this day and age the problem is less of a problem. When you observe the sides of these buildings they glitter and shine as gold, yet they are very transparent from the inside. This is just speculation, but John would describe the wall in terms with which he was familiar.

Rev21:19 And <2532> the foundations <2310> of the wall <5038> of the city <4172> were garnished with <2885> (5772) all manner of <3956> precious <5093> stones <3037>. The first <4413> foundation <2310> was jasper <2393>; the second <1208>, sapphire <4552>; the third <5154>, a chalcedony <5472>; the fourth <5067>, an emerald <4665>;

Rev21:20 The fifth <3991>, sardonyx <4557>; the sixth <1623>, sardius <4556>; the seventh <1442>, chrysolite <5555>; the eighth <3590>, beryl <969>; the ninth <1766>, a topaz <5116>; the tenth <1182>, a chrysoprasus <5556>; the eleventh <1734>, a jacinth <5192>; the twelfth <1428>, an amethyst <271>.

We commonly use the word "garnished" in respect to food. It's a thin ring of something special at the base the main item. And here it is a ring of gems that circumscribes the parameter of each floor. It is left to the reader to assign whatever signifigance that may be indicated by the various gems. Some relate each gem with its color. As such it would provide an ornate feature to each floor as well as beauty to the structure in general.

21 And <2532> the twelve <1427> gates <4440> were twelve <1427> pearls <3135>; every <1538> <303> several <1520> gate <4440> was <2258> (5713) of <1537> one <1520> pearl <3135>: and <2532> the street <4113> of the city <4172> was pure <2513> gold <5553>, as it were <5613> transparent <1307> glass <5194>.

The pearl only has significance as given by God to the Body of Christ. It is His "Pearl of great price" which He communicated in the Mystery Parables of Matthew 13. Though the gates were named with the name of the tribes of Israel, the description of each gate was that of a pearl. The Old Testament conveys Israel's value of numerous gems, but, the pearl wasn't one of them. The name of the tribe on a specific gate had to do with those without, but the pearl at every gate had to do with those within.

Rev21:22 And <2532> I saw <1492> (5627) no <3756> temple <3485> therein <1722> <846>: for <1063> the Lord <2962> God <2316> Almighty <3841> and <2532> the Lamb <721> are <2076> (5748) the temple <3485> of it <846>.

No temple! For Israel, the temple was the very center of their culture. Israel will always have a temple.

In the book of Ezekiel, chapters 39 thru 48 we have the revelation of a temple. The description of it's construction and function is preceded with the same phrase that we have seen in Revelation 21, "it is done" and given a definite designation in time, "in that day". It is not the intent of this book to exposit Ezekiel's temple. It is essential to show that though there is no temple in the New Jerusalem and there is a millennium temple on earth.

Eze 39:8 Behold, it is come <0935> (8804), and it is done <01961> (8738), saith <05002> (8803) the Lord <0136> GOD <03069>; this is the day <03117> whereof I have spoken <01696> (8765).

It is well, to note that the body of Christ had no temple, it was a temple.

1Co 6:19 What <2228>? know ye <1492> (5758) not <3756> that <3754> your <5216> body <4983> is <2076> (5748) the temple <3485> of the Holy <40> Ghost <4151> which is in <1722> you <5213>, which <3739> ye have <2192> (5719) of <575> God <2316>, and <2532> ye are <2075> (5748) not <3756> your own <1438>?

1Pe 2:5 Ye <846> also <2532>, as <5613> lively <2198> (5723) stones <3037>, are built up <3618> (5743) a spiritual <4152> house <3624>, an holy <40> priesthood <2406>, to offer up <399> (5658) spiritual <4152> sacrifices <2378>, acceptable <2144> to God <2316> by <1223> Jesus <2424> Christ <5547>.

In the New Jerusalem, the Lord God Almighty and the Lamb are the temple in it. It would seem repetitious to labor the identities here. There are no physical characteristics here, just persons that built the Body of Christ uniquely for themselves and their own purpose.

Lighting in the New Jerusalem

Rev21: 23 And <2532> the city <4172> had <2192> (5719) no <3756> need <5532> of the sun <2246>, neither <3761> of the moon <4582>, to <2443> shine <5316> (5725) in <1722> it <846>: for <1063> the glory <1391> of God <2316> did lighten <5461> (5656) it <846>, and <2532> the Lamb <721> is the light <3088> thereof <846>.

Now as to the lighting. I AM the light of the world and God is light, are familiar phrases. Here we find that the Lamb is the actual perceivable light to the New Jerusalem interior. Essentially the sun is replaced by the Son. There was a preview on the mount of transfiguration.

Mt 17:2 And <2532> was transfigured <3339> (5681) before <1715> them <846>: and <2532> his <846> face <4383> did shine <2989> (5656) as <5613> the sun <2246>, and <1161> his <846> raiment <2440> was <1096> (5633) white <3022> as <5613> the light <5457>.

Have you ever wondered if when the High Priest entered the Holy of Holies, did he take a torch with him? No, because the glory of God abode there. The walls were of pure gold and light from the world was absent. But the glory of God departed in the book of Ezekiel. Not God, but the glory of God. No little man made box would contain God. We see here the new location of the Glory of God and the Lamb in a square shaped structure not make by human hands.

Eze 10:18 Then the glory <03519> of the LORD <03068> departed <03318> (8799) from off the threshold <04670> of the house <01004>, and stood <05975> (8799) over the cherubims <03742>.

Eze 10:19 And the cherubims <03742> lifted up <05375> (8799) their wings <03671>, and mounted up <07426> (8735) from the earth <0776> in my sight <05869>: when they went out <03318> (8800), the wheels <0212> also were beside <05980> them, and every one stood <05975> (8799) at the door <06607> of the east <06931> gate <08179> of the LORD'S <03068> house <01004>; and the glory <03519> of the God <0430> of Israel <03478> was over them above <04605>.

Rev21: 24 And <2532> the nations <1484> of them which are saved <4982> (5746) shall walk <4043> (5692) in <1722> the light <5457> of it <846>: and <2532> the kings <935> of the earth <1093> do bring <5342> (5719)

their <846> glory <1391> and <2532> honour <5092> into <1519> it <846>.

Where are these "saved nations"? Well, they are not said to be in the New Jerusalem, so it reasons that they are on the New earth. The Old Testament make it clear that Israel would not be the only nation to be included in the Millennium. Psalms 2 speaks of a king in Zion and now we have the Lord in the New Jerusalem and the activity is ruling the nations. It would appear that not only is the Lamb the interior lighting of the New Jerusalem, but provides the lighting of the New earth also. Understand that the New Jerusalem has no night, which means as a unit there is not time, but eternity. The new earth, with some redeemed and future souls to be redeemed, would still require the same conditions of light, day and night, and time as the Body of Christ had previous to the rapture. It further states that the kings (plural) who are on the earth and are outside the New Jerusalem bring their glory and honor into it. So for those who are qualified, have valid credentials and can satisfy the angels at the gate, will be admitted.

Nations have kings and kings have accountability also. It's hard to prove that in history, but the accounting hasn't taken place yet. Now we get some enlightenment as to why the New Jerusalem has gates and guards. Kings bring their glory and honor into it. Its starting to look like the Bride will be receiving company. So much for the impractical "harp on the cloud" thing and more like a practical functioning entity is the order of the day.

Rev21:25 And <2532> the gates <4440> of it <846> shall <2808> <0> not <3364> <0> be shut <2808> (5686) at all <3364> by day <2250>: for <1063> there shall be <2071> (5704) no <3756> night <3571> there <1563>.

Unlike the New Earth, the New Jerusalem doesn't have any night or time clock. The capability of those on earth would have access on a full time basis. That would be like our Romans 5:2 situation.

Rev21:26 And <2532> they shall bring <5342> (5692) the glory <1391> and <2532> honour <5092> of the nations <1484> into <1519> it <846>.

I'm glad to see that I'm not the only one that is prone to repetition. If there is something new here I missed it. As men harvests grain, here it is as if the Lord harvests glory and honor.

Rev21:27 And <2532> there shall <1525> <0> in no wise <3364> enter <1525> (5632) into <1519> it <846> any thing <3956> that defileth <2840> (5723), neither <2532> whatsoever worketh <4160> (5723) abomination <946>, or <2532> maketh a lie <5579>: but <1508> they which are written <1125> (5772) in <1722> the Lamb's <721> book <975> of life <2222>.

This explains why the angels on the gates. There are exclusive areas of the temple in the New Earth which are exclusively holy and restricted, but not all. The New Jerusalem is totally holy and the requirement for entry is absolute. It would seem that only those with an "eternal status "would be admitted.

Revelation, Chapter 22

Rev22:1   And <2532> he shewed <1166> (5656) me <3427> a pure <2513> river <4215> of water <5204> of life <2222>, clear <2986> as <5613> crystal <2930>, proceeding <1607> (5740) out of <1537> the throne <2362> of God <2316> and <2532> of the Lamb <721>.

John now is shown another feature, a river of water of life. The river is common to us as is the water. God is life, I am the Way, the Truth and the life, I came that you may have life, are again familiar phrases. However, it is apparent that light and life are taking on a totally unique substantive reality. The shocking reality for man is that what was just words on a page has become substance and reality. "I am" was vague to Moses. It was defined and clarified in the Incarnate Christ and now it is absolute. There is absolute truth whether man agrees or not. So much for options! The water was clear as crystal, just like its source. Intentional corruption of our present water supply is a deplorable reality, but the solution will not be found in man's ecology programs. The Bride (the Body of Christ) was used to water and it should be no surprise that it's a big feature in our new environment. If we remember the revelation of the first man before the fall and his environment, then why would we think that our new environment would be so different? The water is not only clear as crystal, but unique, a water of life. The word for life is not that which is common to the old creation, but "zoe" that which is used of the life principle of God himself. It is said to proceed out of the throne of God and of the Lamb. What ever it is, it is not still but flowing. Again, everything good, pure, crystal clear proceeds from a source of the same origin. The important principle from the Old Testament that "you can't get a pure thing out of an unpure thing". Also it is coming from a seat of authority. God (the overarching authority) and the Lamb (the specific authority) set the order and focus point of the river.

Rev22: 2 In <1722> the midst <3319> of the street <4113> of it <846>, and <2532> on either <2532> side <1782> <1782> of the river <4215>, was there the tree <3586> of life <2222>, which bare <4160> (5723) twelve <1427> manner of fruits <2590>, and yielded <591> (5723) her <846> fruit <2590> every <2596> <1538> <1520> month <3376>: and <2532> the leaves <5444> of the tree <3586> were for <1519> the healing <2322> of the nations <1484>.

This is a guess, but we have islands in the Mississippi, so why not in the river of life. Anyway in its center and on the banks a familiar tree is growing. It is interesting that access to the tree is only by way of crossing the river. Below are 3 verses relative to that tree. It grew in the Garden of Eden and was prohibited to fallen man. They (Adam & Eve) didn't break the prohibition of this tree, but they did partake of the tree of the knowledge of good and evil. God graciously expelled them from the garden and posted guards so they could not make their fallen estate permanent. The tree of the knowledge of good and evil is nowhere in our text and that issue has been taken care of by the Person and work of our Savior. The tree of life is once again attainable on God's terms.

Ge 2:9 And out <04480> of the ground <0127> made <06779> <00> the LORD <03068> God <0430> to grow <06779> (8686) every tree <06086> that is pleasant <02530> (8737) to the sight <04758>, and good <02896> for food <03978>; the tree <06086> of life <02416> also in the midst <08432> of the garden <01588>, and the tree <06086> of knowledge <01847> of good <02896> and evil <07451>.

Ge 3:22 And the LORD <03068> God <0430> said <0559> (8799), Behold <02005>, the man <0120> is become as one <0259> of us, to know <03045> (8800) good <02896> and evil <07451>: and now, lest he put forth <07971> (8799) his hand <03027>, and take <03947> (8804) also of the tree <06086> of life <02416>, and eat <0398> (8804), and live <02425> (8804) for ever <05769>:

Ge 3:24 So he drove out <01644> (8762) the man <0120>; and he placed <07931> (8686) at the east <06924> of the garden <01588> of Eden <05731> Cherubims <03742>, and a flaming <03858> sword <02719> which turned every way <02015> (8693), to keep <08104> (8800) the way <01870> of the tree <06086> of life <02416>.

Like everything else God creates, this tree provides a unique purpose. It is a tree of life (zoe life). Not a bio life, subject to disease and corruption, but a life akin to the Source. It is said to be fruit bearing every month with twelve different kinds of fruit. Again, the word "fruit" is that which is common to our understanding. It doesn't state who gets the fruit, but it does state that the leaves are for the healing of the nations. A pharmacy to the New Earth, so we can see another reason for their coming to the New Jerusalem.

Rev22:3 And <2532> there shall be <2071> (5704) no <3756> more <2089> <3956> curse <2652>: but <2532> the throne <2362> of God <2316> and <2532> of the Lamb <721> shall be <2071> (5704) in <1722> it <846>; and <2532> his <846> servants <1401> shall serve <3000> (5692) him <846>:

Like the tree of the knowledge of good and evil, our contribution, the curse due to our sin, is omitted. We, of all people can say, "free at last, free at last, praise God Almighty we're free at last" and declare it truthfully. Now, not free to serve self, but that which has been invested in us and worked out during our earthly pilgrimage, free to serve and love in the fullness of heart Him who first loved and served us. The suffering Servant, the Lord Jesus. Again, Heaven will not be a place of inactivity for the Body of Christ. The bread of idleness is not in the New Jerusalem. If serving the Lord on the old earth seemed like a unwanted chore, then an examination of your salvation is probably in order. There is no greater joy for the child than to work with his Father. God has presented himself as a builder and person of purpose. Now He has made us joint-heirs in Christ. Now because of our being, not doing, we are not spectators, but real participants.

Rev22:4 And <2532> they shall see <3700> (5695) his <846> face <4383>; and <2532> his <846> name <3686> shall be in <1909> their <846> foreheads <3359>.

No longer as thru a glass darkly, but face to face with my redeemer. My first tendency will be to draw back, but then I'll recount the wonder of my Savior and the perfection of his perfect work in my behalf. The closest I can come now is to worship him in spirit and truth and to know his presence. Corporately, it is the high point of the week. I've heard it said that service to God without His presence is vanity and I've found that to be true. The error of ministry in this age is that the emphasis is place on doing to establish our being. If we establish our being first, then the next stage is worship and from worship to service. In the eastern translation of the word service (latraou) is translated worship. Then, Joshua can be heard to say, "for me and my household, we will worship the LORD. In this era we commonly preach and praise, but we don't worship as set forth in the Scripture. Were we to place those who "worship, in spirit and in truth" in their rightful place, the inflated congregations would be greatly diminished and the Body of Christ less liked and more respected?

We will be identified with him.

1John 3:2 Beloved <27>, now <3568> are we <2070> (5748) the sons <5043> of God <2316>, and <2532> it doth <5319> <0> not yet <3768> appear <5319> (5681) what <5101> we shall be <2071> (5704): but <1161> we know <1492> (5758) that <3754>, when <1437> he shall appear <5319> (5686), we shall be <2071> (5704)

like <3664> him <846>; for <3754> we shall see <3700> (5695) him <846> as <2531> he is <2076> (5748).

Far better than those who took the mark of distinction from Satan, we are identified not by a mark, but by being like Him. Granted we have unknown details, but to be like Him makes all else insignificant. Anyway what ever is unknown will be a temporary condition. When he appears we will see Him as he is, face to face.

Rev22:5 And <2532> there shall be <2071> (5704) no <3756> night <3571> there <1563>; and <2532> they need <5532> no <3756> candle <3088> <2192> (5719), neither <2532> light <5457> of the sun <2246>; for <3754> the Lord <2962> God <2316> giveth <5461> <0> them <846> light <5461> (5719): and <2532> they shall reign <936> (5692) for <1519> ever <165> and ever <165>.

We have experienced the "reign of sin", been delivered at Calvary from its reign over us by the Shed Blood in the presence of sin and now we will reign apart from the element of sin. Scripture tell us how long that will be for Body of Christ.

1Th 4:17 Then <1899> we <2249> which <3588> are alive <2198> (5723) and remain <4035> (5742) shall be caught up <726> (5691) together <260> with <4862> them <846> in <1722> the clouds <3507>, to <1519> meet <529> the Lord <2962> in <1519> the air <109>: and <2532> so <3779> shall we <2071> <0> ever <3842> be <2071> (5704) with <4862> the Lord <2962>.

Marriage is forever in the New Jerusalem, where the Husband goes, so goes the Bride. The Body of Christ and its Head were presented separately in time, but now as the Bride of Christ any separation is gone forever. We know little of what happens after the final accounting at the end of the Millennium, and those redeemed in the New Earth. What we do know is that our place and relationship with the Lamb is immutable. Our only need is the Son. Again, we are not spectators. We shall reign with Him as joint-heirs and that eternally. Praise the Lord!

6 And <2532> he said <2036> (5627) unto me <3427>, These <3778> sayings <3056> are faithful <4103> and <2532> true <228>: and <2532> the Lord <2962> God <2316> of the holy <40> prophets <4396> sent <649> (5656) his <846> angel <32> to shew <1166> (5658) unto his <846> servants <1401> the things which <3739> must <1163> (5748) shortly <1722> <5034> be done <1096> (5635).

And so we come to the closing parenthesis of the revelation on the New Jerusalem. These sayings are faithful and true. It opens with Rev 21:5 and closes at Rev 22:6. It is a directive from the Lord God of the holy prophets and delivered by his angel to reveal to his servants the things which must shortly be done. It is well to remember that the setting has not changed since the 4th Chapter of Revelation. The Lord and the Holy prophets have not changed from the Old Testament and this text simply completes the instruction to Israel. It presently is informative to the Body of Christ. "Shortly" (without delay) for the Body of Christ the meaning is immanent and for Israel some 7 years plus after the snatching away of the Body of Christ. From God's view the basis of redemption of man in any age was finished at Calvary. Here he makes it clear that from his view all the elements necessary to fulfill his intent, "to make all things new" are completed.

Intermission for summing up of Heaven for the Body of Christ

Having reviewed the text of Rev 21 & 22, it should now be able to get a Scriptural view of Heaven as it pertains to the Body of Christ. It should dispel the false notions that have lingered in the past. That will include not only the ethereal which subtracts from Scripture by saying nothing to the "way out" speculations which add the hallucinations of the fleshly mind. Heaven is a practical, purposeful, functional abode for a select group of redeemed men to serve a God Man in the completion of his great design. The concept that its condition will be largely different than of his original design of man is erroneous. The Lord Jesus took on the form of man that He might reveal Himself to better work with man. Now we, as the Body of Christ, are privileged to work with Him, as interns, in the behalf of those functioning in the continued worship and redemption of men on the New Earth in the millennium. What is so confusing about that?

After such a review, a coherent picture of future events and the ones particular to the Body of Christ and the New Jerusalem should have emerged. If that has not happened, or if the given text and references are of no interest, then there is a much greater issue for the reader.

The picture is presented here in common language. With the knowledge that God is making all new components to assemble into one new functioning unit and that the old ones are vanished and to be remembered no more, lets look at the picture. Understand that all the parts come together at the same juncture and will complement each other during the millennium. That juncture, then, has to be at the end of the period known as the Great Tribulation, Jacob's Sorrows or the 70th week of Daniel.

On the New Earth the Purified Israel, the Jews, will live in accord with all that God promised them. David will get his throne, Ezekiel his temple, a new form of the gospel will be in effect, their children will be candidates for salvation, day, night and time will continue and conditions will be "thy Kingdom come, on earth as it is in heaven". God will be with, his people, Israel. They and the redeemed nations will have access and accountability at the New Jerusalem.

Suspended between heaven and earth is the New Jerusalem. In present day terms, it is a satellite. It is the abode of the Bride of Christ (Body of Christ), the Lord Jesus the Christ (the Head) and the Glory of God.

The function of worship of God there is more of substance and with one heart and one mind. That is "The mind of Christ". His body will aid and administer the purposes of their Lord and love Him forever. There is little detail of the functions within the New Jerusalem, however why should it be so different from that of life as previously experienced. The Body of Christ was a body of priest. As previously stated, the New Jerusalem complements the New Earth and those living on it.

Nothing is said of how travel between the two entities is accomplished other than what was exhibited by our Lord when he was here. We know for certain that Scripture confirms that travel to and from the New Earth for some is certain. Gravity would not seem to be an issue.

It is a city. The construction would be most likely a cubehaving transparent side walls. Each side is said to be approximately 1500 miles. A lesser wall would surround the main structure at its base with 3 gates per side each identified with the name of a tribe of Israel. Each gate is said to resemble a pearl. A jeweled garnish having a unique color is around each side at the structures foundations (floors) and makes it look like a jewel box. Reminds one of the urim and thummim. The interior construction is similar to a 12 story building, each story bearing the name of a disciple. The Lords throne is there from which issues a river of living water. Unique vegetation is present and probably much of what one might have seen in the Garden of Eden, like the tree of Life.

Lighting is a primary feature. The Lord provides the light within it, but also without to light the New Earth. Those on earth are said to walk in that light. There is no night there but day and night continue on the New Earth. The material structure seems to make that a reality. The lighting of the New Earth provides the time cycles just as the old sun did.

The function to those who enter from the New Earth is said to bring their glory and honor into it. Again, it is worship and accountability. It also seems to serve as some kind of a pharmacy.

It is a closed city, that is to say entrance is limited to those qualified. Angels administer the security at each gate and nothing is said of their position other than that they are outside the city at each gate. Maybe like Cherabim at the Garden of Eden. In this case they are to insure that no contamination enters the city. The primary function of angels in Scripture is that which is related to Israel.

That's our picture of heaven according to Scripture with a few minor comments included. The point is that Scripture says it, not man. Whether man likes it or not, it is as valid as any other part of Scripture. No one gets to pick and chose. Like the Law, it is all or nothing.

There is a great value of knowing where the Body of Christ is going. It is a great motivation to "study to show yourself approved" and experience the ministry of a priest. He promised rest and this portion of Scripture provides just that. My spirit will show you all things and so he has. The darkness is dispelled and we can rest in his revelation.

The rest of the instruction to Israel

Note: actually the intent of this book has be met. It seemed that from this point, I, as the author, could just rely on the exposition of those who have covered the area quite thoroughly in the past. However, the element of conviction seems to reject that course. Most of what has been exposited comes from those with a previous stage of revelation and so I will continue with that which corresponds with the revelation of this present time.

By now the reader should have noted that the sequence of events in the time line differ from the common tradition. Any concept that proposes that the New Jerusalem appears at any other time than immediately following the Great Tribulation has serious contextual and time problems. What goes on in the Millennium is interdependent with the functions of the New Jerusalem. They have to exist at the same time.

Given that that is true, the remaining text of Revelation 22 has some translation of words which render it in a non harmonious way. This mistranslation destroys the original intent by bringing in concepts that do not pertain to this element of God's design. Granted that some valid concepts and translations are valid in their proper scriptural place, but to force them in this text is to confuse the revelation of what God intended to communicate.

Rev 22: 7 Behold <2400> (5628), I come <2064> (5736) quickly <5035>: blessed <3107> is he that keepeth <5083> (5723) the sayings <3056> of the prophecy <4394> of this <5127> book <975>.

The Lord commands his subjects attention and informs them that He is coming without delay. The question that becomes apparent is "to whom is he coming?". He has said, "it is done" relative to the Body of Christ. Doubtless they are all ready in the New Jerusalem and know of His movements. Knowledge of the prophecies will be useful to the Body of Christ as it functions in the New Jerusalem during the Millennium, but for them the content of this verse is of no consequence. His process moves to the next stage where the "all things new" come together in the Millennium and the persons requiring this information are those who will enter into the Millennium. There is nothing in Scripture that states that such persons will be indwelt by the Holy Spirit, so such a command would indeed be necessary. The blessing is a state of being for those who keep all the prophecies, not some, but all, who ever they are. The Nestle/ Marshall translation says "keeping" for keep and "words" for sayings. Either way, it is clear that the intent is that such knowledge is to be maintained. Revelation 22:10 adds additional detail on the restrictions, or lack of restriction, and time of application.

Rev 22:8 And <2532> I <1473> John <2491> saw <991> (5723) these things <5023>, and <2532> heard <191> (5723) them. And <2532> when <3753> I had heard <191> (5656) and <2532> seen <991> (5656), I fell down <4098> (5627) to worship <4352> (5658) before <1715>

the feet <4228> of the angel <32> which <3588> shewed <1166> (5723) me <3427> these things <5023>.

John saw and heard and it moved him to action. What are the "these things" referred two twice? It is noteworthy that he didn't say "this thing". The "things" are plural. So it is evident that John now refers to all that the angel has shown him and having completed his revelation of the New Jerusalem, he moves back to include "these things" that is, all that John has seen.

As previous stated the angel ministry is scripturally confined to Israel and if at all to the Body of Christ, to those to be saved. There is and has been since the 4th Chapter, an angel ministry and save for the Revelation of the Bride of Christ, no involvement of the Body of Christ.

For anyone that has experienced God's working, the action resulting is quite predicable, worship. Such experiences also bring with them an overwhelming of ones person and so John's action of misdirected worship seems quite human. Vary shortly John will be giving instruction to the angels.

Rev 22:9 Then <2532> saith he <3004> (5719) unto me <3427>, See <3708> (5720) thou do it not <3361>: for <1063> I am <1510> (5748) thy <4675> fellowservant <4889>, and <2532> of thy <4675> brethren <80> the prophets <4396>, and <2532> of them which keep <5083> (5723) the sayings <3056> of this <5127> book <975>: worship <4352> (5657) God <2316>.

The angel sets John straight by rejecting his worship and gives us a means of his identity. He, the angel, is as the word describes,a messenger. The word brethren defined in both the Old and New Testament is "from the same womb". The angel is of thy brethren of the prophets and keeps the words of the book. Again, the identity is to prophets. Granted that Eph 4 speaks of personified gifted persons called prophets, but it is not likely that these are the prophets referred to here. John knew what prophets the angel was talking about and they were not in the New Testament. The Body of Christ was still a mystery. If otherwise, the angel would have identified with the Apostles. John's worship is redirected.

If you haven't understood it by now, the intent of mentioning about angels and prophets is to make it clear that John's present setting has nothing to do with the New Jerusalem or the Body of Christ. The setting here and as we proceed with the text is on Israel's ground.

Rev 22:10 And <2532> he saith <3004> (5719) unto me <3427>, Seal <4972> (5661) not <3361> the sayings <3056> of the prophecy <4394> of this <5127> book <975>: for <3754> the time <2540> is <2076> (5748) at hand <1451>.

Daniels instruction was just the opposite of that given to John.

Da 9:24 Seventy <07657> weeks <07620> are determined <02852> (8738) upon thy people <05971> and upon thy holy <06944> city <05892>, to finish <03607> (8763) the transgression <06588>, and to make an end <08552>

(8687) (8675) <02856> (8800) of sins <02403>, and to make reconciliation <03722> (8763) for iniquity <05771>, and to bring in <0935> (8687) everlasting <05769> righteousness <06664>, and to seal up <02856> (8800) the vision <02377> and prophecy <05030>, and to anoint <04886> (8800) the most <06944> Holy <06944>.

Da 12:4 But thou, O Daniel <01840>, shut up <05640> (8798) the words <01697>, and seal <02856> (8798) the book <05612>, even to the time <06256> of the end <07093>: many <07227> shall run to and fro <07751> (8787), and knowledge <01847> shall be increased <07235> (8799).

The question is now "what book is he referring to?". In Daniel's case it didn't affect the rest of the Old Testament. Some have said that, here in Revelation, "the book" could cover the whole of Scripture. As God is the author of both statements, it is most probable that he meant the same thing, past and present.

In the years, 1960 and before, the Book of the Revelation and Daniel, its counterpart in the Old Testament, was a closed portion of scripture. It was, in the case of Daniel, sealed. The book of the revelation might just as well been sealed. Some like Uriah Smith (1897) and William Kelly (1901) stayed with the literal text, but for the most part it was perverted or ignored by most Bible Scholars. Now it is "front and center". The idea of satellites and space travel in the past was the stuff for the comics. Not so today, the text and the application meet. At the present time we have manned space stations and some 22,000 man made items orbiting our planet. So what's so odd about God making the New Jerusalem a satellite. It should be abundantly obvious that he has created a universe of such suspended objects.

For those who are familiar with scripture, it is an established truth that there is a time table for Israel. That is not the case for the Body of Christ. With Israel there is a set schedule, milestones, days and exact dates are given. So it is here, the time is at hand. It's not some arbitrary floating time, the time is right on schedule. Through the word for time used here is "chairos" and it speaks largely of the character of an interval, it is the word our Lord used when deriding Israelites because they didn't know what time it was.

Mt 16:2 <1161> He answered <611> (5679) and said <2036> (5627) unto them <846>, When it is <1096> (5637) evening <3798>, ye say <3004> (5719), It will be fair weather <2105>: for <1063> the sky <3772> is red <4449> (5719).

Mt 16:3 And <2532> in the morning <4404>, It will be foul weather <5494> to day <4594>: for <1063> the sky <3772> is red <4449> (5719) and lowring <4768> (5723). O ye hypocrites <5273>, ye can <1097> (5719) discern <1252> (5721) <3303> the face <4383> of the sky <3772>; but <1161> can ye <1410> (5736) not <3756> discern the signs <4592> of the times <2540>?

Rev22:11 He that is unjust <91> (5723), let him be unjust <91> (5657) still <2089>: and <2532> he which is filthy <4510> (5723), let him be filthy <4510> (5657) still <2089>: and <2532> he that is righteous <1342>, let him be righteous <1344> (5682) still <2089>: and <2532> he that is holy <40>, let him be holy <37> (5682) still <2089>.

We commonly say, "the die is cast". The "He" states that all persons are now in a fixed state. Just as the "new" is complete, the old is "frozen". The purified Israelites proceed into the Millennium and the rest are rejected. This is very like when the Body of Christ was complete and removed from the earth. There will be no additions to the Body of Christ. Behold the goodness and severity of the Lord! Whatever the state, good or bad, change is now out of the question for those He is addressing. For the Body of Christ that was established at the Bema.

At this point it is commonly understood that His coming is that of the Great White throne and to judge men for their works. Let's take a closer look. We have already reviewed the first phrase of verse 12 in verse 7, so we won't repeat that.

Rev22:12 And <2532>, behold <2400> (5628), I come <2064> (5736) quickly <5035>; and <2532> my <3450> reward <3408> is with <3326> me <1700>, to give <591> (5629) every man <1538> according as <5613> his <846> work <2041> shall be <2071> (5704).

"My reward" is referenced in Psalm 127:3. As those in the Body of Christ were referred to as children of Light, so there are those children redeemed in Israel, some having been martyred in the Tribulation.

Rev6:9 And <2532> when <3753> he had opened <455> (5656) the fifth <3991> seal <4973>, I saw <1492> (5627) under <5270> the altar <2379> the souls <5590> of them that were slain <4969> (5772) for <1223> the word <3056> of God <2316>, and <2532> for <1223> the testimony <3141> which <3739> they held <2192> (5707):

Rev6:10 And <2532> they cried <2896> (5707) with a loud <3173> voice <5456>, saying <3004> (5723), How <2193> long <4219>, O Lord <1203>, holy <40> and <2532> true <228>, dost thou <2919> <0> not <3756> judge <2919> (5719) and <2532> avenge <1556> (5719) our <2257> blood <129> on <575> them that dwell <2730> (5723) on <1909> the earth <1093>?

Rev6: 11 And <2532> white <3022> robes <4749> were given <1325> (5681) unto every one of them <1538>; and <2532> it was said <4483> (5681) unto them <846>, that <2443> they should rest <373> (5672) yet <2089> for a little <3398> season <5550>, until <2193> their <846> fellowservants <4889> also <2532> and <2532> their <846> brethren <80>, that should <3195> (5723) be killed <615> (5745) as <5613> <2532> they <846> were, should <3739> be fulfilled <4137> (5695).

Ps 127:3 Lo, children <01121> are an heritage <05159> of the LORD <03068>: and the fruit <06529> of the womb <0990> is his reward <07939>.

In Rev22:9 the angel said that he was "of the brethren the prophets". In the Old testament the word brethren is used 629 times and in the New Testament, 346 times.

Either place it is define as "from the same womb". Note that "Christian" is only used in scripture twice in a history book. So if "his reward" and "my reward" are both pertaining to the Lord and are the same, they appear to be peoplethat return with him. Rev20:4 says that "I saw thrones and them that sat upon them". Could they, in fact, be his reward that returns with him.

What kind of judgement is this? Lets look at Scripture and let scripture define scripture.

Isa40:9 O Zion <06726>, that bringest good tidings <01319> (8764), get thee up <05927> (8798) into the high <01364> mountain <02022>; O Jerusalem <03389>, that bringest good tidings <01319> (8764), lift up <07311> (8685) thy voice <06963> with strength <03581>; lift it up <07311> (8685), be not afraid <03372> (8799); say <0559> (8798) unto the cities <05892> of Judah <03063>, Behold your God <0430>!

Isa40:10 Behold, the Lord <0136> GOD <03069> will come <0935> (8799) with strong <02389> hand, and his arm <02220> shall rule <04910> (8802) for him: behold, his reward <07939> is with him, and his work <06468> before <06440> him.

Isa40:11 He shall feed <07462> (8799) his flock <05739> like a shepherd <07462> (8802): he shall gather <06908> (8762) the lambs <02922> with his arm <02220>, and carry <05375> (8799) them in his bosom <02436>, and shall gently lead <05095> (8762) those that are with young <05763> (8802).

Does verse Isa 40:10, in context sound like Rev 20:11?

Rev20:11 And <2532> I saw <1492> (5627) a great <3173> white <3022> throne <2362>, and <2532> him that sat <2521> (5740) on <1909> it <846>, from <575> whose <3739> face <4383> the earth <1093> and <2532> the heaven <3772> fled away <5343> (5627); and <2532> there was found <2147> (5681) no <3756> place <5117> for them <846>.

Rev20: 12 And <2532> I saw <1492> (5627) the dead <3498>, small <3398> and <2532> great <3173>, stand <2476> (5761) before <1799> God <2316>; and <2532> the books <975> were opened <455> (5681): and <2532> another <243> book <975> was opened <455> (5681), which <3739> is <2076> (5748) the book of life <2222>: and <2532> the dead <3498> were judged <2919> (5681) out of <1537> those things which were written <1125> (5772) in <1722> the books <975>, according to <2596> their <846> works <2041>.

Or does it sound like Rev 20:4?

Rev20:4 And <2532> I saw <1492> (5627) thrones <2362>, and <2532> they sat <2523> (5656) upon <1909> them <846>, and <2532> judgment <2917> was given <1325> (5681) unto them <846>: and <2532> I saw the souls <5590> of them that were beheaded <3990> (5772) for <1223> the witness <3141> of Jesus <2424>, and <2532> for <1223> the word <3056> of God <2316>, and <2532> which <3748> had <4352> <0> not <3756> worshipped <4352> (5656) the beast <2342>, neither <3777> his <846> image <1504>, <2532> neither

<3756> had received <2983> (5627) his mark <5480> upon <1909> their <846> foreheads <3359>, or <2532> in <1909> their <846> hands <5495>; and <2532> they lived <2198> (5656) and <2532> reigned <936> (5656) with <3326> Christ <5547> a thousand <5507> years <2094>.

It's pretty obvious that Rev 22:12 is not the White Throne Judgment. "To give to every man" is in harmony with God's common mode of justice. "According as his work shall be" tells us that it is a "works" judgment, but note what is not said. The works are not said to all bad. It is just like the Bema judgment for the Body of Christ. Now if even human generated good works are as filthy rags, this judgment would be for bad works only and it clearly is not. There is no negative connotation here. The statement does imply that the "works" have occurred in a system of law as was true in Israel. It will also be true in the Millennium.

What ever that is, it is to be given to every man according as his work shall be. Compare this with I Cor 3:16.

1Cor:11 For <1063> other <243> foundation <2310> can <1410> (5736) no man <3762> lay <5087> (5629) than <3844> that is laid <2749> (5740), which <3739> is <2076> (5748) Jesus <2424> Christ <5547>.

1Cor: 12 Now <1161> if any man <1536> build <2026> (5719) upon <1909> this <5126> foundation <2310> gold <5557>, silver <696>, precious <5093> stones <3037>, wood <3586>, hay <5528>, stubble <2562>;

13 Every man's <1538> work <2041> shall be made <1096> (5695) manifest <5318>: for <1063> the day <2250> shall declare <1213> (5692) it, because <3754> it shall be revealed <601> (5743) by <1722> fire <4442>; and <2532> the fire <4442> shall try <1381> (5692) every man's <1538> work <2041> of what sort <3697> it is <2076> (5748).

1Cor: 14 If any man's <1536> work <2041> abide <3306> (5719) which <3739> he hath built <2026> (5656) thereupon, he shall receive <2983> (5695) a reward <3408>.

1Cor:15 If any man's <1536> work <2041> shall be burned <2618> (5691), he shall suffer loss <2210> (5701): but <1161> he himself <846> shall be saved <4982> (5701); yet <1161> so <3779> as <5613> by <1223> fire <4442>.

This would be the Bema judgment for the Body of Christ and has already transpired prior to the judgment spoken of here.

Rev 22:13 I <1473> am <1510> (5748) Alpha <1> and <2532> Omega <5598>, the beginning <746> and <2532> the end <5056>, the first <4413> and <2532> the last <2078>.

In the first part of this book the topic of Theology Proper was mentioned. Again, it is the revelation of God of himself. It was not then or is it here the intent to present same. In this verse, God makes the all encompassing statement relative to himself at the end of his design. All that he has and will create starts and finishes with Him.

"I" the person, "I am" as the state of being and the content and confines are given here. Moses wanted to know who was sending him and He responded:

Ex 3:14 And God <0430> said <0559> (8799) unto Moses <04872>, I AM <01961> (8799) THAT I AM <01961> (8799): and he said <0559> (8799), Thus shalt thou say <0559> (8799) unto the children <01121> of Israel <03478>, I AM hath sent <07971> (8804) me unto you.

In the incarnation, the Lord Jesus presented himself as the "I am's" of the Gospels, but He was rejected by his own when he came to his own. Now speaking to the purified Israel, He presents himself to those who once corporately rejected him. He is their Messiah in every extent. As the Alpha and Omega He comprises the elements of words and the words,if truly composed, speak of all He is, intends, and creates, including Israel. It all starts and ends with Him. Initially the picture that comes to mind with the beginning and the end is that of a straight line, but as one grows in grace and the knowledge of him that image changes to something like a ball of string that has no end. In the New Testament he, the Lord Jesus is presented as the prototype. That is, the first of the kind. Adam failed in that rite when tested, but Jesus of Nazareth did not. To the Body of Christ he was the first to run the course successfully and establish the way for them to follow. Now, he is the last of his kind.

Eph 2:15 Having abolished <2673> (5660) in <1722> his <846> flesh <4561> the enmity <2189>, even the law <3551> of commandments <1785> contained in <1722> ordinances <1378>; for to <2443> make <2936> (5661) in <1722> himself <1438> of twain <1417> one <1519> <1520> new <2537> man <444>, so making <4160> (5723) peace <1515>;

Though many will be redeemed during the Millennium on earth, there will be no more men redeemed in the configuration of those in the Body of Christ.

To say what could be said or should be said is beyond this person's capability. Isaiah probably said it best.

Isa 9:6 For unto us a child <03206> is born <03205> (8795), unto us a son <01121> is given <05414> (8738): and the government <04951> shall be upon his shoulder <07926>: and his name <08034> shall be called <07121> (8799) Wonderful <06382>, Counsellor <03289> (8802), The mighty <01368> God <0410>, The everlasting <05703> Father <01>, The Prince <08269> of Peace <07965>.

Rev 22: 14 Blessed <3107> are they that do <4160> (5723) his <846> commandments <1785>, that <2443> they <846> may have <2071> (5704) right <1849> to <1909> the tree <3586> of life <2222>, and <2532> may enter <1525> (5632) in through the gates <4440> into <1519> the city <4172>.

We now have the promise based on a legal condition, "do and receive". The persons being addressed are in a law condition and are blessed by doing his commandments, not just hearing or believing, but doing. This provides them the right to have access to the tree of Life and to enter in through the gates of "the city". What this tells us is that they are living outside the New Jerusalem where the tree of Life is. The means of access is through the gates of said city. Previously we learned where the tree of Life is, where the city is and about the gates for accessing same. Without laboring the point further, these person live on the New Earth and gain access to the tree of life in the New Jerusalem by the "pearly gates".

Rev22: 15 For <1161> without <1854> are dogs <2965>, and <2532> sorcerers <5333>, and <2532> whoremongers <4205>, and <2532> murderers <5406>, and <2532> idolaters <1496>, and <2532> whosoever <3956> loveth <5368> (5723) and <2532> maketh <4160> (5723) a lie <5579>.

Thought the New Earth will initially be populated with redeemed people and be in an ideal state, they will populate the New Earth with lost souls. If one studies the features of the earth in the Millennium they will find that said features are not so different from those on the old earth during Israel's former existence where redemption is concerned. The earthly temple, the sacrifices, a form of law & grace and many more are present and functional. As such, only qualified persons will be able to pass into the eternal state inside the New Jerusalem. Total Depravity will still exist on the New Earth, but with immediate system of justice.

Rev 22: 16 I <1473> Jesus <2424> have sent <3992> (5656) mine <3450> angel <32> to testify <3140> (5658) unto you <5213> these things <5023> in <1909> the churches <1577>. I <1473> am <1510> (5748) the root <4491> and <2532> the offspring <1085> of David <1138>, and the bright <2986> and <2532> morning <3720> star <792>.

Again, we have the "I" of personhood. The name Jesus is of Hebrew origin and as such could be Joshua. It would complement the context better. Jesus = "Jehovah is Salvation". Any way it is not his Lordship or his title, the Christ. It is the man, Jesus. He states that he, the man, sent his angel to testify "these things". Again we have the question of what are "these things" and to whom are they to be testified. Now we come to a word that neither fits its primary definition or the context in which it appears. The word is church. I distain to use the word "church" and more so the image it conjures up in the mind. How we got such a word is a long story and what is said to constitute a "church" in the modern era is even more deplorable. The word can be anything the speaker conjures up in his mind. The listener ignores the word as meaningless or creates his own definition and image in his own mind. The "devil being in the details" all is well if they communicate nothing, but results in chaos when it becomes clear that the images of the speaker and the listener don't match. So in this verse let us use ekklesia as God intended. It is not unique to the Body of Christ or the New Testament. It has a variety of definition, but basically it is defined as" a called out assembly of people", so let us use it that way and omit the false image created by fleshly mistranslation. Back to our text and to those in the Millennium. The angel's instruction is to testify to the called out assemblies. This brings harmony and sense to the verse with that which contextually came before and that which follows. It also eliminates the snare of preconceived notions.

Again, "I am" is the root and the offspring of David. For those in the Body of Christ, David, the Davidic Covenant and King David really don't seem that important. That is especially true when one considers where they are when this statement is fulfilled. To Israel, it is everything. It establishes authority from their origin to this statement.

Here He is established as the "root".

Joh 8:58 Jesus <2424> said <2036> (5627) unto them <846>, Verily <281>, verily <281>, I say <3004> (5719) unto you <5213>, Before <4250> Abraham <11> was <1096> (5635), I <1473> am <1510> (5748).

Here He is the "offspring".

Lu 2:11 For <3754> unto you <5213> is born <5088> (5681) this day <4594> in <1722> the city <4172> of David <1138> a Saviour <4990>, which <3739> is <2076> (5748) Christ <5547> the Lord <2962>.

Here we see Him as the Servant of Jehovah.

Isa53:2 For he shall grow up <05927> (8799) before <06440> him as a tender plant <03126>, and as a root <08328> out of a dry <06723> ground <0776>: he hath no form <08389> nor comeliness <01926>; and when we shall see <07200> (8799) him, there is no beauty <04758> that we should desire <02530> (8799) him.

Here we have Him at his 2nd coming. The key phrase is "in that day".

Isa11:10 And in that day <03117> there shall be a root <08328> of Jesse <03448>, which shall stand <05975> (8802) for an ensign <05251> of the people <05971>; to it shall the Gentiles <01471> seek <01875> (8799): and his rest <04496> shall be glorious <03519>.

Isa11:11 And it shall come to pass in that day <03117>, that the Lord <0136> shall set <03254> <00> his hand <03027> again <03254> (8686) the second time <08145> to recover <07069> (8800) the remnant <07605> of his people <05971>, which shall be left <07604> (8735), from Assyria <0804>, and from Egypt <04714>, and from Pathros <06624>, and from Cush <03568>, and from Elam <05867>, and from Shinar <08152>, and from Hamath <02574>, and from the islands <0339> of the sea <03220>.

Isa11:12 And he shall set up <05375> (8804) an ensign <05251> for the nations <01471>, and shall assemble <0622> (8804) the outcasts <01760> (8737) of Israel <03478>, and gather together <06908> (8762) the dispersed <05310> (8803) of Judah <03063> from the four <0702> corners <03671> of the earth <0776>.

Here He functions in the Millennium.

Isa27: 6 He shall cause them that come <0935> (8802) of Jacob <03290> to take root <08327> (8686): Israel <03478> shall blossom <06692> (8686) and bud <06524> (8804), and fill <04390> (8804) the face <06440> of the world <08398> with fruit <08570>.

Isa37: 31 And the remnant <07604> (8737) that is escaped <06413> of the house <01004> of Judah <03063> shall again <03254> (8804) take root <08328> downward <04295>, and bear <06213> (8804) fruit <06529> upward <04605>:

Here He identifies himself as "the bright and Morning Star". To those living on the New Earth that may be more of an actuality that just a statement.

Moses saw Him afar off in a function of judgment as a star.

Nu 24:17 I shall see <07200> (8799) him, but not now: I shall behold <07789> (8799) him, but not nigh <07138>: there shall come <01869> (8804) a Star <03556> out of Jacob <03290>, and a Sceptre <07626> shall rise <06965> (8804) out of Israel <03478>, and shall smite <04272> (8804) the corners <06285> of Moab <04124>, and destroy <06979> (8773) all the children <01121> of Sheth <08352> (8676) <08351>.

2Pet1:19 We have <2192> (5719) also <2532> a more sure <949> word <3056> of prophecy <4397>; whereunto <3739> ye do <4160> (5719) well <2573> that ye take heed <4337> (5723), as <5613> unto a light <3088> that shineth <5316> (5730) in <1722> a dark <850> place

<5117>, until <2193> <3739> the day <2250> dawn <1306> (5661), and <2532> the day star <5459> arise <393> (5661) in <1722> your <5216> hearts <2588>:

Psalm 2 is a familiar psalm and clearly takes place in the Millennium.

Rev2:27 And <2532> he shall rule <4165> (5692) them <846> with <1722> a rod <4464> of iron <4603>; as <5613> the vessels <4632> of a potter <2764> shall they be broken to shivers <4937> (5743): even <2504> <0> as <5613> I <2504> received <2983> (5758) of <3844> my <3450> Father <3962>.

Rev2:28 And <2532> I will give <1325> (5692) him <846> the morning <4407> star <792>.

Rev2:29 He that hath <2192> (5723) an ear <3775>, let him hear <191> (5657) what <5101> the Spirit <4151> saith <3004> (5719) unto the called out assemblies <1577>.

Rev22:17 And <2532> the Spirit <4151> and <2532> the bride <3565> say <3004> (5719), Come <2064> (5628). And <2532> let him that heareth <191> (5723) say <2036> (5628), Come <2064> (5628). And <2532> let him that is athirst <1372> (5723) come <2064> (5628). And <2532> whosoever will <2309> (5723), let him take <2983> (5720) the water <5204> of life <2222> freely <1432>.

We now have an invitation from two entities, the first being the Holy Spirit and the second the Bride of Christ.

To establish their location we have only to remember that the residence of the Bride of Christ is the New Jerusalem, so it is an invitation from that location. That the Holy Spirit would give such an invitation is not unusual. What is different is that it is no longer the Lord Jesus giving the invitation.

Mt 11:28 Come <1205> (5773) unto <4314> me <3165>, all <3956> ye that labour <2872> (5723) and <2532> are heavy laden <5412> (5772), and I <2504> will give <373> <0> you <5209> rest <373> (5692).

The task at hand is the salvation of men in the Millennium. The nature of His function would be much like it was on the old earth as a regenerator, a revelator and actualizer.

Eph1:13 In <1722> whom <3739> ye <5210> also <2532> trusted, after that ye heard <191> (5660) the word <3056> of truth <225>, the gospel <2098> of your <5216> salvation <4991>: in <1722> whom <3739> also <2532> after that ye believed <4100> (5660), ye were sealed with <4972> (5681) that holy <40> Spirit <4151> of promise <1860>,

Eph1:14 Which <3739> is <2076> (5748) the earnest <728> of our <2257> inheritance <2817> until <1519> the redemption <629> of the purchased possession <4047>, unto <1519> the praise <1868> of his <846> glory <1391>.

Joh 16:8 And <2532> when he is come <2064> (5631), he <1565> will reprove <1651> (5692) the world <2889> of

<4012> sin <266>, and <2532> of <4012> righteousness <1343>, and <2532> of <4012> judgment <2920>:

Now we see from a different perspective something of the function of the Bride. The text doesn't say, but we can assume that since the two give the invitation jointly that they are involved in the same function. That function is the redemption of those people who are born in the Millennium.

The substance of the invitation, the gospel of the Millennium, will be unique to the conditions of the era. What that is exactly is not stated, but what we know is that the basis of that gospel has not changed. It is the finished work of Christ.

And let him that heareth say, come. We have those subjects who hear responding. It sound much like it was for the Body of Christ that without Divine enablement there is no response. The repeating of the substance of the message, "come" is repeated back and works much like the function in the word "confession". The hearer responds and agrees with the source.

And let him that is athirst, come. As it was on the old earth there is a void, an appetite that requires satisfying. The problem is that what it takes to satisfy the thirst is not on earth.

And whosoever will, let him take of the water of life, freely. Again, as it was on the old earth there is a "meeting of the wills" and when that is the case, we have a person who can gain admission to the New Jerusalem where the water of life is. The spirit and the Bride called from the New Jerusalem and the person is to respond and come.

The word "freely" means just what it always means when one is the object of the Lord's salvation.

Joh 8:36 If <1437> the Son <5207> therefore <3767> shall make <1659> <0> you <5209> free <1659> (5661), ye shall be <2071> (5704) free <1658> indeed <3689>.

Rev22:18 For <1063> I testify <4828> (5736) unto every man <3956> that heareth <191> (5723) the words <3056> of the prophecy <4394> of this <5127> book <975>, If <1437> any man <5100> shall add <2007> (5725) unto <4314> these things <5023>, God <2316> shall add <2007> (5692) unto <1909> him <846> the plagues <4127> that are written <1125> (5772) in <1722> this <5129> book <975>:

Rev22:19 And <2532> if <1437> any man <5100> shall take away <851> (5725) from <575> the words <3056> of the book <976> of this <5129> prophecy <4394>, God <2316> shall take away <851> (5692) his <846> part <3313> out of <575> the book <976> of life <2222>, and <2532> out of <1537> the holy <40> city <4172>, and <2532> from the things which are written <1125> (5772) in <1722> this <5026> book <975>.

In verses 18 & 19 we have a stern warning to the hearers. The warning concerns "the prophecy of this book". Again, as it was with the "sealing" issue, the warning is probably confined to Revelation alone. It alone has the plagues and persons capable of being the subject of such actions

This can't pertain to the Bride of Christ or volumes of Scripture are contradicted. It therefore must pertain to those who will use Scripture after the Body of Christ has become the Bride of Christ.

Again, the thing not to be changed is the "prophecy". What is the prophecy of this book? It is clearly that which pertains to the last week of Israel's history, the 70th week of Daniel, the great tribulation or Jacob's sorrow and the revelation of the New Jerusalem, its relation to Earth and occupants.

The "adding to or subtracting from" is to those who know Him self explanatory. Whether it is to this book, 66 books or any word in Scripture, the message from an Immutable God is, "no change" and if you do, it will come to an accounting and unspeakable consequences.

In the New Testament era the exposition of the Scriptures has been universally covered. There is, however, an avoiding of the Scripture exposited in Chapters 21 & 22 of this book. Maybe it is because God has not illumined it and spiritual men can't see it. More likely they do see it and seek to avoid the stark realities of God's intent. Emotion becomes the motivator, not Scripture. Facing the doctrine of election is not going to be without its problems. In short, men aren't going to like it.

The harsh reality is that regardless of whether we understand, agree or not with God, his plan will prevail, unchanged. The obligation of man is to, as the hymn says, "trust and obey, not pass judgment. We have reached that point in God's plan when the man's lies, white or otherwise, can no longer hide the reality of the coming events.

In Noah's day this was true and 8 souls were saved and approximately 40 million perished. God didn't ask permission then and he won't when the New Heaven and Earth become a reality. What is the capacity of the New Jerusalem? What is the present population of the earth? If the ratio of saved to perished remains anywhere constant the volume of the perishing is going to be quite large. Such questions do make one draw back and question God. What happened to the "loving" God? He is just as he has presented himself—Holy, Just, Righteous, and loving. Our problem is that we are making ourselves god and neglecting what was directly assigned to us. Preaching a simple gospel and maturing those He saves. What happens to the lost is His matter and His alone. Why did God give this revelation if it didn't intend it an essential part of our education. He gave us His Spirit to teach us all of his Revelation, so let's do it.

Rev22:20 He which testifieth <3140> (5723) these things <5023> saith <3004> (5719), Surely <3483> I come <2064> (5736) quickly <5035>. Amen <281>. Even so <3483>, come <2064> (5736), Lord <2962> Jesus <2424>.

What is here has been covered previously with the exception of that which appears to be missing. The title of "Christ" is missing. What is the significance of that is, if any, is unknown. We know that repeated phrases and words make the statement more intense. His human name preceded by the authoritative word "Lord" would seem to declare his position and authority to those to whom he is speaking.

Phil2:10 That <2443> at <1722> the name <3686> of Jesus <2424> every <3956> knee <1119> should bow <2578> (5661), of things in heaven <2032>, and <2532> things in earth <1919>, and <2532> things under the earth <2709>;

Phil2:11 And <2532> that every <3956> tongue <1100> should confess <1843> (5672) that <3754> Jesus <2424> Christ <5547> is Lord <2962>, to <1519> the glory <1391> of God <2316> the Father <3962>.

Rev22:21 The grace <5485> of our <2257> Lord <2962> Jesus <2424> Christ <5547> be with <3326> you <5216> all <3956>. Amen <281>.

John closes with the universal characteristic of His design, Grace. It stems from the Source that we addressed at the inception of His design and continues to its conclusion. It stands on the foundation of his Lordship, his humanity and his title, all righteously attained through his conception, construction and completion of one grand design.

Commentary of Rev 22:7
thru Rev 22:21

Having seen the Bride, John, in the presence of one of the angels, is brought to a state of worship. At first it is miss directed toward the angel, but that was short lived as the angel made it clear that they both served the same master. The angel that had been active in the purification of Israel had a break in his duties to show John the Bride and the New Jerusalem. He, the angel, having finished with that task resumes to issues that pertain directly to Israel and states that the state of things, mainly persons, is now permanently fixed.

If it is possible to consider a "time line" or a depiction of the relative positions, the Body of Christ is already the Bride of Christ residing in the New Jerusalem. From this point in the text the angel's duties now pertain to persons that have been purified and entered into the Millennium.

The Lord becomes the speaker to these persons and announces his coming and purpose. He introduces himself. A blessed state with conditions to achieve that state are provided along with access to the Tree of Life that now resides in the New Jerusalem. In contrast with that blessed estate is the knowledge that the New Earth is still subject to the same conditions that were present on the Old Earth. The rituals and sacrifices in the temple would still be required. The Lord makes it clear that this information is to be circulated in the assemblies. He establishes him self as having existed before King David and having lived as a man under his reign, that he is now King David's Lord reigning from the New Jerusalem.

The purpose of redemption on the New Earth that is in "ideal condition" is now activated. The Spirit and the Bride are the primary initiators and invite those who hear, thirst and will to partake of the water of life freely.

The good news was the blessing and the bad news is the warning for failing to strictly adhere to the prophecy of this book. Psalm 2 makes that abundantly clear.

The Lord again states of his coming without delay and seals it with "so be it".

He notes the character of his reign and closes with his full signature.

The Lord Jesus the Christ.

Conclusion

In the end, heaven is not so mystical after all. It would be strangely inconsistent to create and develop people only to place them in some foreign condition doing something undefined for which they had not been trained. This present earth is in a corruptible state created by man. God is simply "making all things new" without the corruption and to accomplish his original intent. However, it is like the Epistle to the Hebrews describes, immensely better.

About the Author

A 74 year old man, husband of one wife, one daughter (graduate of Emmaus Bible College).

Education: Self taught–Due to a medical defect. High school Graduate--Academic.

Professional: Progressed from Draftsman 1956 to Mech. Design Project Engineer 1978 (11 years) Presently Retired.

Military: 6 year obligation in United States Marine Corps 1958-1964. Honorable Discharge.

Elder and founder: Grace Bible Chapel, Highland, IL 62249–15 years.

Christian ministry--------Volunteer-in-Probation, Orange, CA—4 Years.

Free lance Missions in Mexico (primarily prisons)—6 years , IL prisons(Fed&State) 4 years.

Theological education: 3 years in intense, word for word study thru the New Testament in Greek.

Complete study of Systematic Theology—Louis Sperry Shafer, and too many volumes to mention.

Christian orientation: Brethren by Scripture, that is, having finished study of Scriptures that was the inductive conclusion and conviction.